COLLABORATIONS: ENGLISH IN OUR LIVES

INTERMEDIATE 2 WORKBOOK

Jean Bernard
Donna Moss
Lynda Terrill

AF530917

Heinle & Heinle Publishers
A Division of International Thomson Publishing, Inc.
Boston, MA 02116, U.S.A.

The ITP logo is a trademark under license.

The publication of *Collaborations* was directed by the members of the Heinle & Heinle Secondary and Adult ESL Publishing Team:

Editorial Director: Roseanne Mendoza
Senior Production Services Coordinator: Lisa McLaughlin

Also participating in the publication of the program were:

Vice President and Publisher ESL: Stanley Galek
Associate Developmental Editor: Sally Conover
Production Editor: Maryellen Killeen
Manufacturing Coordinator: Mary Beth Hennebury
Full Service Design and Production: PC&F, Inc.
Illustration Program: Brian Karas, Michael Johnston, and PC&F, Inc.

Copyright © 1997 by Heinle & Heinle Publishers

All rights reserved. No part of this publication may be reproduced or transmitted in any form or by any means, electronic or mechanical, including photocopying, recording, or any information storage and retrieval system, without the permission in writing from the publisher.

Manufactured in the United States of America.

ISBN: 0-8384-6635-4

03 02 01 00 99 – 7 6 5 4 3

Heinle & Heinle is a division of International Thomson Publishing, Inc.

Photo Credits:

Cover: © Jonathan Stark/Heinle & Heinle

Unit 1: Jean Bernard, 1, 2, 5, 7, 9, 11; David Moss, 4; Mariano Ramos Hernandez (book cover), 10.

Unit 2: Jeanne H. Schmedlen, 15, 16, 19 top left, 23; Corpus Christi Literacy Council, 17; Betty Lynch, 19 top right; Thai-Hung Pham Nguyen, 21.

Unit 3: David Moss, 27, 28, 30, 31, 32, © Jonathan Stark/Heinle & Heinle, 36; Jean Bernard, 36.

Unit 4: Greater Corpus Christi Business Alliance, 39; David Moss, 40, 49; Betty Lynch, 46.

Unit 5: Alan McGee/FPG, 53; David Moss, 54, 56, 59, 62.

Unit 6: Jean Bernard, 67, 68, 73, 74, 75, 76, 78.

BRIEF CONTENTS • • •

Unit 1 **Maintaining Cultural Traditions** in Connecticut 1

Unit 2 **Sharing Strategies** in Harrisburg, Pennsylvania 15

Unit 3 **Dating and Marriage** in Washington, D.C. 27

Unit 4 **Finding Success** in Corpus Christi, Texas 39

Unit 5 **Special Communities** Refugees in Comer and Atlanta, Georgia 53

Unit 6 **Staying in Touch** Stories from Laos and California 67

Answer Key 81

The *Collaborations Intermediate 2 Workbook* accompanies the *Collaborations Intermediate 2 Student Book.* This workbook is designed to reinforce the vocabulary, lifeskills, grammar, reading skills, and writing skills from the student book. Each unit opens with a list of page numbers from the student book correlated to those in the workbook unit. This serves as a guide to students and instructors. Because the workbook is designed for self-study situations, it can be used in the classroom by students working with the instructor or by students working independently.

CONTENTS • • •

Unit 1 Maintaining Cultural Traditions in Connecticut 1

Vocabulary Review: Words and Phrases to Describe People 2
Grammar Review: Subject Complements After *Be* 3
Grammar Review: Relative Clauses About People 4
More Reading and Writing: More About the Puerto Rican Experience 5–6
Vocabulary Review: Personal Talents 7
Study Skills and Strategies: Taking Notes 8
Grammar Review: Preposition Clusters 9
Grammar Review: Passive Voice Verbs, Past and Present 10
Study Skills and Strategies: Supporting Opinions 11
Doint It in English: Reporting Cultural Identity 12
Test Yourself 13
Language Learning Diary 14

Unit 2 Sharing Strategies in Harrisburg, Pennsylvania 15

Vocabulary Review: Educational Strategies 16
Study Skills and Strategies: Paraphrasing 17
Grammar Review: Past Perfect Continuous 18
Doing It in English: Expressing Need 19
Grammar Review: Using Base Words and Affixes 20
Study Skills and Strategies: Using Context to Guess Meanings 21
Vocabulary Review: Figures of Speech 22
More Reading and Writing: More Learning Strategies from Harrisburg 23
Doing It in English: Using Media for Focused Listening 24
Test Yourself 25
Language Learning Diary 26

Unit 3 Dating and Marriage in Washington, D.C. 27

Study Skills and Strategies: Inferring 28
Vocabulary Review: Using Phrasal Verbs 29
Grammar Review: Reported Speech 30
More Reading and Writing: Chet Kong's Story 31
Vocabulary Review: Describing Personal Characteristics 32
Doing It in English: Making and Responding to Invitations 33
Doing It in English: Reading a News Report 34
Study Skills and Strategies: Reading Graphs 35
Grammar Review: Parts of Speech 36
Test Yourself 37
Language Learning Diary 38

Unit 4 **Finding Success in Corpus Christi, Texas** 39

Vocabulary Review: Describing Work Skills 40
Grammar Review: Embedded Questions 41
Study Skills and Strategies: Writing a Personal Data Sheet 42–43
Doing It in English: Filling Out a Job Application 44–45
More Reading and Writing: More About Delilah Flores 46–47
Vocabulary Review: Job and Career Titles 48
Grammar Review: Subject-Verb Agreement 49
Grammar Review: Agreeing, Disagreeing, and Being Unsure 50
Test Yourself 51
Language Learning Diary 52

Unit 5 **Special Communities** Refugees in Comer and Atlanta, Georgia 53

Grammar Review: Writing Wh- Questions 54
Vocabulary Review: Describing Places 55
More Reading and Writing: Nermina Silnovic's Story 56
Grammar Review: Asking for Help 57
Doing It in English: Opening a Bank Account 58–59
Doing It in English: Filling Out Health Forms 60
Study Skills and Strategies: Reading Tables 61
Study Skills and Strategies: Using Transition Words 62–63
Study Skills and Strategies: Outlining a Speech to Inform 64
Test Yourself 65
Language Learning Diary 66

Unit 6 **Staying in Touch** Stories from Laos and California 67

Vocabulary Review: Ways of Staying in Touch 68
Doing It in English: Sending International Mail 69–70
Study Skills and Strategies: Recognizing Levels of Formality in Writing 71–72
Grammar Review: Using Conditional Sentences 73
Grammar Review: Expressing Wishes 74
Study Skills and Strategies: Adding Factual Information 75
Study Skills and Strategies: Recognizing Time and Sequence Clues 76
More Reading and Writing: *Native Country:* Memories of Vietnam 77
Vocabulary Review: Major Life Events 78
Test Yourself 79
Language Learning Diary 80

Answer Key 81

Unit 1 Maintaining Cultural Traditions in Connecticut

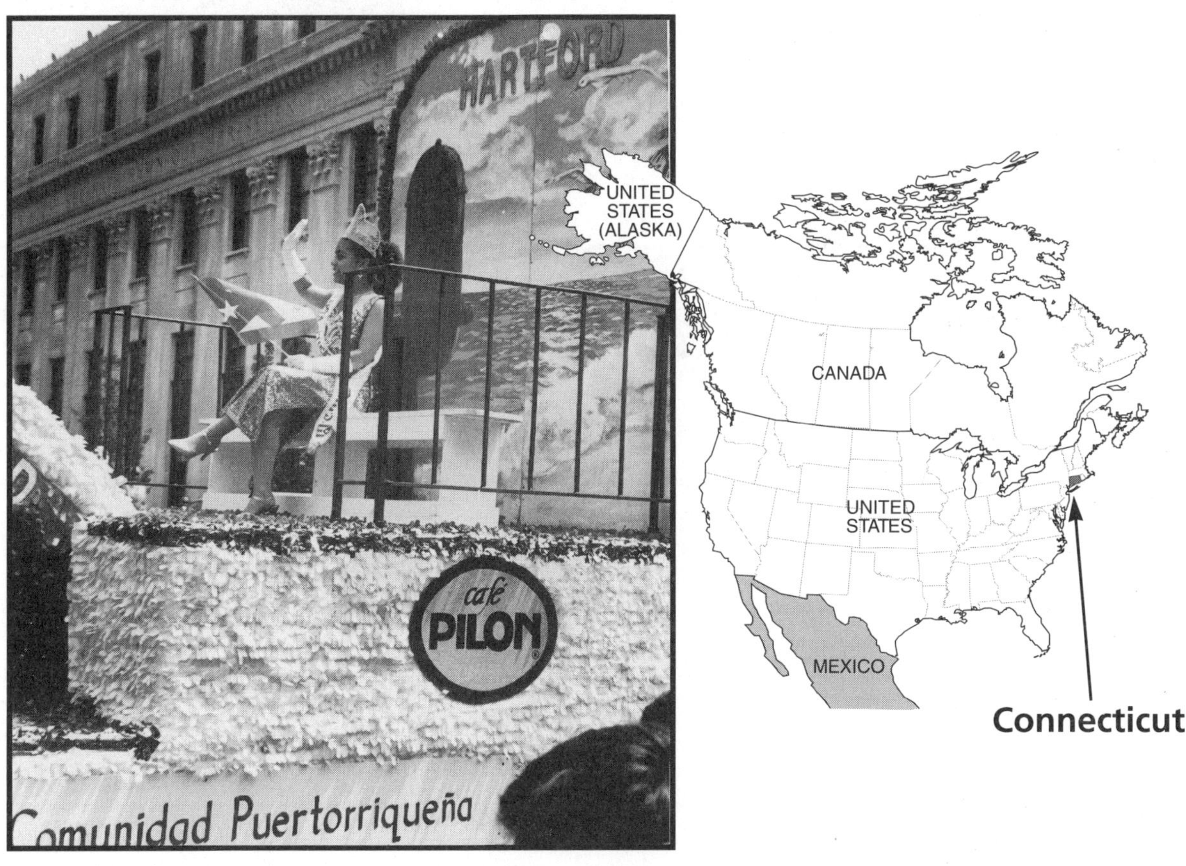

When to Do Your Workbook Pages

Page		Do after Student Book Page
1	**Overview**	
2	**Vocabulary Review** Words and Phrases to Describe People	4
3	**Grammar Review** Subject Complements After *Be*	5
4	**Grammar Review** Relative Clauses About People	5
5–6	**More Reading and Writing** More About the Puerto Rican Experience	6
7	**Vocabulary Review** Personal Talents	7
8	**Study Skills and Strategies** Taking Notes	7
9	**Grammar Review** Preposition Clusters	8
10	**Grammar Review** Passive Voice Verbs, Past and Present	10
11	**Study Skills and Strategies** Supporting Opinions	11
12	**Doing It in English** Reporting Cultural Identity	14
13	**Test Yourself**	15
14	**Language Learning Diary**	15

Vocabulary Review: Words and Phrases to Describe People

A. Read the words and phrases Mariano Ramos Hernandez used to describe himself. Do any of the same words describe you? Check (✔) "yes" or "no." If you chose "no," write a word or phrase that describes you.

Mariano Ramos	Me? Yes	No	Words and Phrases That Describe Me
a lucky guy			
poor			
humble			
happy			
an original			
Puerto Rican			
a Catholic			
proud of who I am			
retired			

B. Look at the diagram below. In the center oval, write words and phrases that describe both you and Mariano Ramos. Write the ones that describe *only* Mariano on the left. Complete the right side of the diagram with words and phrases that describe you, but not Mariano. Add as many more as you wish.

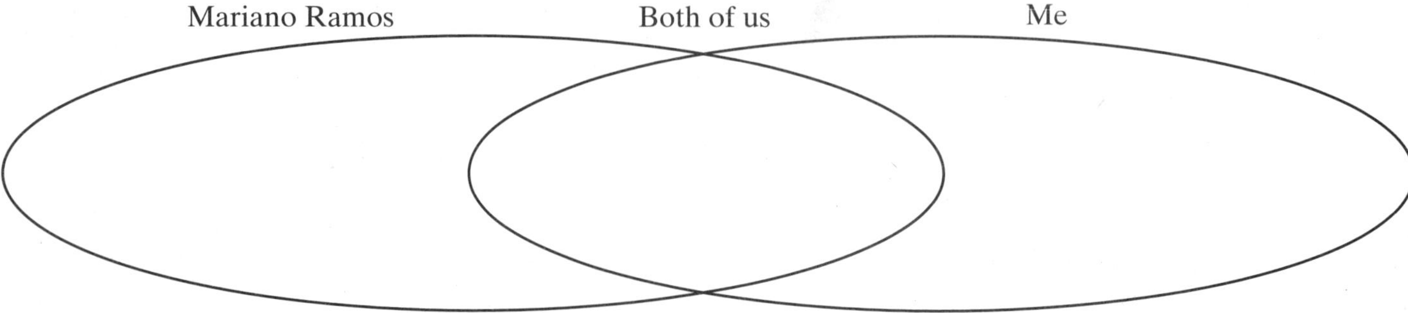

Grammar Review: Subject Complements After *Be*

A. Read more about Mariano Ramos Hernandez. Underline all forms of the verb *to be*, and circle each subject complement.

> I have been a hard worker all my life. Now that I am retired, I spend a lot of time writing poetry. To tell you the truth, I am still a very busy man. I am president of the Puerto Rican Poets' Society, and I work with the elderly two days a week. My poems are pretty well known in Latino communities. The poem called "Carbonero" is especially popular.

Subject Complements
After any form of the verb *be,* use a noun, a noun phrase, or an adjective.
He's always been a poet. I'm not rich, but I'm healthy and strong.

B. Rewrite each of the sentences below, keeping close to the same meaning. Use a form of the verb *to be* and a verb complement from the story in each sentence.

Example:

He has worked hard all his life.

He has been a hard worker.

1. He doesn't have to work for a living now.

____

2. He doesn't have much free time.

____

3. Many people in Latino communities know his poems.

____

C. Complete each of the sentences about yourself. Write one or more words in each space.

1. I have always been ________________________.

2. Now that I am ____________ I spend a lot of time ____________.

3. I am ____________ of ____________.

4. My ____________ is (are) ____________.

Grammar Review: Relative Clauses About People

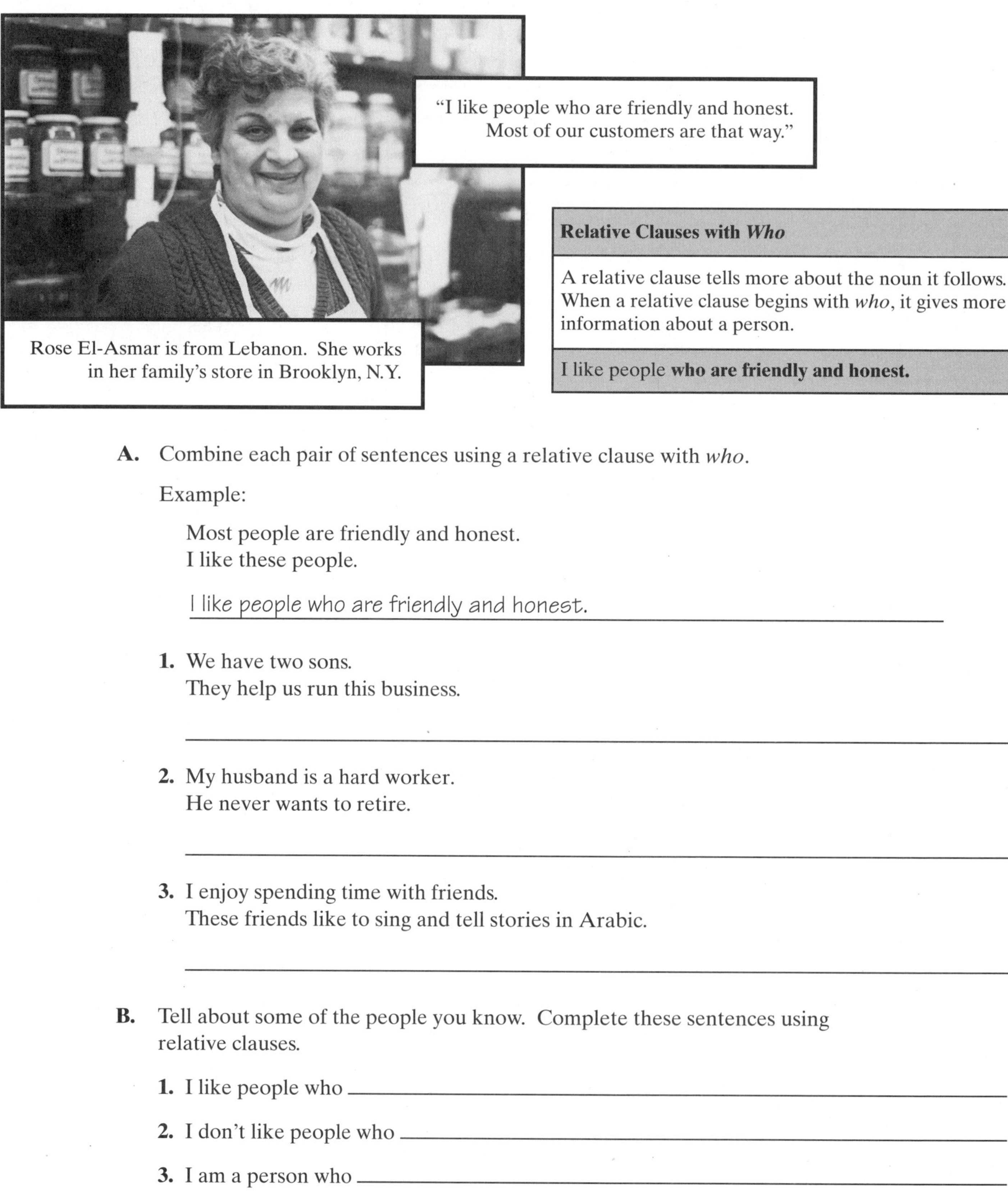

"I like people who are friendly and honest. Most of our customers are that way."

Rose El-Asmar is from Lebanon. She works in her family's store in Brooklyn, N.Y.

Relative Clauses with *Who*
A relative clause tells more about the noun it follows. When a relative clause begins with *who*, it gives more information about a person.
I like people **who are friendly and honest.**

A. Combine each pair of sentences using a relative clause with *who*.

Example:

Most people are friendly and honest.
I like these people.

I like people who are friendly and honest.

1. We have two sons.
They help us run this business.

____

2. My husband is a hard worker.
He never wants to retire.

____

3. I enjoy spending time with friends.
These friends like to sing and tell stories in Arabic.

____

B. Tell about some of the people you know. Complete these sentences using relative clauses.

1. I like people who ______________________________.

2. I don't like people who ______________________________.

3. I am a person who ______________________________.

4. My best friend is a ________________ who ________________.

More Reading and Writing: More About the Puerto Rican Experience

Puerto Rico is a beautiful island. Whenever I go back there, I always spend some time in the place where I was born and grew up. All of my poetry goes back to that place. I like to walk in the same places I used to go when I was a kid. I put on sandals, a pair of jeans, and a T-shirt. I go to the farms where I used to work, to the house I grew up in.

The house where I was born was a small wooden house with a roof made out of sugar cane leaves. The floor was made of palm tree mats. Later on we moved to another house. They wanted to send me to San Juan to go to a bigger school, but I loved that place. I stayed there until I decided to come to the mainland in 1949.

IDIOMS
have against
our roots
join in

In those days, it wasn't so easy to migrate, even though we Puerto Ricans were citizens of the United States. There were restrictions. We were not allowed to come here just like that. We had to pass through medical examinations, we had to have a sponsor, and we had to swear that we had nothing against the United States government or anything like that.

Now it's easy for us to travel back and forth. Some people say that Puerto Ricans come here to collect welfare, but that is not true. We have contributed a lot toward the building of this nation. We are part of it, we have fought in its wars. The battlefields of Europe, Korea, and Vietnam have been soaked in Puerto Rican blood. It's true that there are a lot of problems in our communities, but for the most part we have a lot to be proud of.

Of course, it's important for us to learn English to get along here, but we don't want to forget our own language, our roots. English is not the only language of the United States, it is a country of many cultures, many languages. It's not fair to discriminate against people because they speak other languages. Really, to tell you the truth, it's not American here. There's no such thing as "American" because we all come from other places.

We have some beautiful traditions. At Christmas time, for example, we celebrate from December 22 to January 7, not just one day and then go back to work. During that period, people often get together to go out into the streets and sing. Let's say this group is going to serenade a certain person. They get the guitars, the *cuatros*[1] and the *maracas*[2] together and go to that house. After they sing a few verses, the owner of the house invites them all in to eat. Then after a while somebody starts in singing again, and everybody else joins in. We often make up new verses as we go.

[1] *cuatro*—a musical instrument with four strings, similar to a guitar

[2] *maraca*—an instrument made of a hollow gourd with beans or small stones inside, usually played in pairs

A. Which part of the story do you think is most interesting?
Circle one topic.

- memories of the author's childhood home
- role of Puerto Ricans in American History
- Puerto Rican migration to the mainland
- opinion on languages spoken in the U.S.
- example of a Puerto Rican cultural tradition

What did you like about the topic you chose? ______________________________

____

____

B. Choose one sentence from the story that you strongly agree or disagree with.
Copy the sentence below.

____

____

Agree or disagree? ____________________

Write your own paragraph explaining why.

____

____

____

____

____

____

____

____

____

____

____

____

Vocabulary Review: Personal Talents

A. What are you good at? Look over the list. Check (✔)the things you are able to do very well. Add more of your own.

The Lam Luang folk opera troupe is based in Providence, R.I. In this photo the actors are performing a traditional folk tale at the Lao Buddhist temple in Manassas, VA.

tell stories	❑	draw	❑
write poetry	❑	take photographs	❑
sing	❑	cook	❑
dance	❑	play soccer	❑
act	❑	____________________	❑
play an instrument	❑	____________________	❑

B. One way to describe personal talents is to use sentences like the one below. In this type of sentence, be sure to add *-ing* to the verb that follows *good at* or *talented at*.

I'm good at drawing and playing soccer, but I'm not very talented at cooking.

Write a sentence or two about your own personal talents.

____

____

____

Write another sentence about someone you know.

____

Study Skills and Strategies: Taking Notes

A. Look at this short biography of Gloria Estefan. Read for general information first.

> Gloria Estefan, the popular Cuban-American singer and songwriter, was born in Havana, Cuba, in 1957. At the age of two, she immigrated with her family to Miami, Florida. She grew up in a house filled with music, both traditional and modern.
>
> After graduating from the University of Miami with a B.A.[1] in Psychology, she started recording her own songs. Her first big success was a song called "Anything for You" (1987). Since then, she has enjoyed tremendous popularity. She appears frequently on MTV[2] and has performed at the Olympics in Seoul, Korea and Atlanta and at the l987 World Series[3].
>
> While she sings mostly in English, her fifth album, "Mi Tierra"[4] (1993) is entirely in Spanish. Estefan is proud of the fact that all of her music is a blend of traditional Cuban music and the sounds of modern rock.

[1]B.A.—Bachelor of Arts
[2]MTV—Music Television, popular music cable channel
[3]World Series—championship series of baseball games played in October
[4]"Mi Tierra"—song title, meaning "my homeland"

B. Which facts about Gloria Estefan are important or interesting to you? Check (✔) the three you would like to remember most.

- ☐ Her date of birth
- ☐ Her country of birth
- ☐ Her age at immigration
- ☐ The city she immigrated to
- ☐ The kinds of music she grew up with
- ☐ The university she graduated from
- ☐ Her first hit song
- ☐ Places she has performed
- ☐ A general description of her music
- ☐ The title of her fifth album

C. Read the article again. In the space below, make notes on the three important points you checked in B. Use as few words and numbers as possible.

> **Learning Strategy**
>
> When you read for information, decide which facts and ideas are important to you. Take notes to help you remember these details.

1. ______________________________

2. ______________________________

3. ______________________________

D. Use your notes to write full sentences about Gloria Estefan without looking back at the article. Write your sentences on a separate sheet of paper.

Grammar Review: Preposition Clusters

A. Look at the photograph. What is the man riding in the parade proud of? Write your answer below the photograph.

____

B. *Proud of* is an example of a **preposition cluster.** Some other preposition clusters are in the box below.

proud, sure, tired, afraid } *of*	pleased, annoyed, comfortable, satisfied } *with*
happy, sad, angry, confused } *about*	good, terrible, lucky, surprised } *at*

Examples:

I'm confused about the directions.
Are you satisified with the answer?
She's lucky at finding good jobs.

Remember that after a preposition cluster, you can use (a) a noun, (b) a gerund phrase, or (c) a noun clause beginning with *what* or *who*.

I'm tired of } my job / working so hard / what people say

C. Choose five different preposition clusters from the box, or use some others that you know. Write a short paragraph about yourself using all five preposition clusters.

____

____

____

____

____

____

Grammar Review: Passive Voice Verbs, Past and Present

This book is called "Desde la Distancia." It was published in 1991.

Passive Voice Verb Forms	
A **passive voice verb form** shows that the subject of a sentence receives the action of the verb. The doer, or performer, of the action may be added (by ________ but is often left out. To form the passive voice, use a form of the verb be + the past participle of the main verb. Most past participles are formed by adding *-ed* to the base verb (see p. 105 of your student book for a list of irregular past participles).	
Active voice (subject performs action)	**Passive voice** (subject receives action)
Lisa *waters* the plants every day. Mariano *published* the book in 1991.	The plants *are watered* every day (by Lisa). The book *was published* in 1991 (by Mariano).

A. Read these statements from Unit 1. Underline the passive verb forms in each sentence.

1. Waterbury is called "The Brass Capital of the World."
2. My first poem was published when I was just eight years old.
3. Puerto Ricans were granted U.S. citizenship in 1917.
4. The Commonwealth of Puerto Rico was established in 1952.
5. Metaphors are used in English to express meaning in interesting ways.

B. Answer the following questions about a poem, a play, or a song you know. If you aren't sure of the exact details, take a guess. Write your answers in complete sentences, beginning each sentence with "It . . ."

1. What is it called?

   ____

2. Who was it written by?

   ____

3. When was it written?

   ____

4. Where was it first published or performed?

   ____

Study Skills and Strategies: Supporting Opinions

A. Which of these statements are facts? Which are opinions? Write F (fact) or O (opinion) next to each statement.

_______ **1.** Connecticut is a small state with a population of about 3,300,000.

_______ **2.** Connecticut is a wonderful place to live.

_______ **3.** Puerto Rico was a colony of Spain until 1898.

_______ **4.** Since the turn of the century, over 2.5 million Puerto Ricans have migrated to Hawaii, New York City, and the New England states.

_______ **5.** Puerto Rican music should be taught in all American schools.

Spectators wait for the Puerto Rican parade in New Haven, Connecticut.

B. When you express an opinion, you can make it stronger by supporting it with facts, examples, or reasons. Look at the examples in the chart.

Opinion	Connecticut is a wonderful place to live.
Reason	I enjoy living in a place where I can hear the sounds of many languages.
Fact	The cities of Hartford, New Haven, and Waterbury have large Latino populations who maintain their cultural traditions in several ways.
Example	The Puerto Rican parade in New Haven is attended by thousands of visitors every year.

C. How do you feel about the place you now live? Write your opinion, then support it with one or more facts, opinions, or examples.

____

____

____

____

____

Doing It in English: Reporting Cultural Identity

A. Many employers and schools in North America use forms like the one below to collect information about applicants' racial and cultural backgrounds. Read the descriptions carefully, and check the one that best fits you.

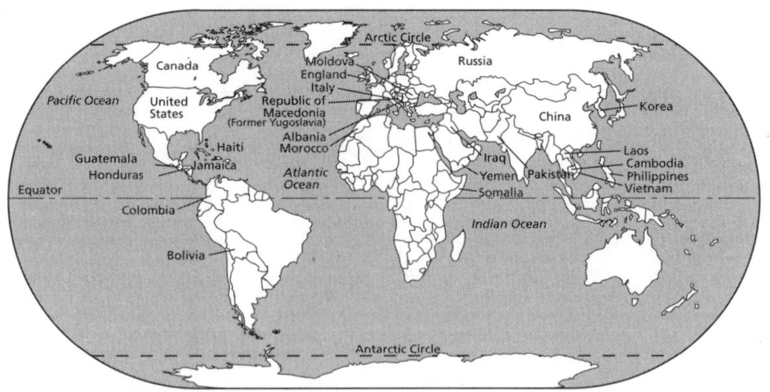

_______ White
A person having origins in any of the original peoples of Europe, North Africa, or the Middle East.

_______ Black
A person having origins in any of the Black racial groups of Africa.

_______ Asian or Pacific Islander
A person having origins in any of the original peoples of the Far East, Southeast Asia, the Indian Subcontinent, or the Pacific Islands. This area includes, for example, China, India, Japan, Korea, the Philippine Islands, and Samoa.

_______ Hispanic
A person of Mexican, Puerto Rican, Cuban, Central or South American culture or any Spanish Culture or origin regardless of race.

_______ American Indian or Alaskan Native
A person having origins in any of the original peoples of North America and who maintains cultural identification through Tribal affiliation or community recognition.

_______ Other*

*If you checked "Other," how would you describe your racial and cultural background?

____

B. Answer the following questions.

1. Have you ever completed a form like this before? Yes ❑ No ❑
2. Completion of this type of form is usually voluntary (you don't have to do it). Do you think it is a good idea to complete the form when you are applying for school or a job? Write "Yes" or "No" and explain your answer.

____

____

____

Test Yourself

Circle or fill in the correct answers.

1. Mariano Ramos Hernandez is proud of who ______________.

   a) he is b) is he c) was he

2. He has a lot more time to write poetry now because he is ______________.

   a) retiring b) retire c) retired

3. Rose El Asmar likes people ______________ are friendly and honest.

   a) who b) whose c) which

4. Her son is good at ______________ stories, but he's not very talented at singing.

   a) tell b) told c) telling

5. Gloria Estefan's first song ______________ "Anything for You."

   a) is calling b) was called c) was call

6. When Mariano returns to Puerto Rico, he always spends some time in the place where he ______________.

   a) was born b) born c) is born

7. When I first arrived, I was confused ______________ the school system.

   a) of b) at c) about

8. Now I understand the way it works, but I'm not always happy ______________ it.

   a) about b) to c) at

9. The Puerto Rican parade ______________ by thousands of people every year.

   a) is attended b) is attending c) attended

10. "Puerto Rico has a population of about 3,522,520" is a(n) ______________.

    a) fact b) opinion c) reason

Language Learning Diary

A. Think about the ways individuals and communities maintain their cultural traditions in a new country **and** about the English you have learned in this unit. Using some of the prompts in the box as guides, write about what you've learned and would like to learn.

I learned about . . .
I spoke English to . . .
I listened to . . .
I read about . . .
I wrote about . . .
The strategies I used are . . .
I want to learn more about . . .

B. New words and phrases I want to remember. Keep a record of when you see, hear, or use a new word or phrase from this unit outside the classroom.

Word/Phrase	I saw it . . .	I heard it . . .	I used it . . .
tradition	in the newspaper	________	at church: I talked with friends

Sharing Strategies
in Harrisburg, Pennsylvania

When to Do Your Workbook Pages

Page		Do after Student Book Page
15	**Overview**	
16	**Vocabulary Review**	
	Educational Strategies	21
17	**Study Skills and Strategies**	
	Paraphrasing	22
18	**Grammar Review**	
	Past Perfect Continuous	23
19	**Doing It in English**	
	Expressing Need	24
20	**Grammar Review**	
	Using Base Words and Affixes	24
21	**Study Skills and Strategies**	
	Using Context to Guess Meaning	25
22	**Vocabulary Review**	
	Figures of Speech	27
23	**More Reading and Writing**	
	More Learning Strategies from Harrisburg	28
24	**Doing It in English**	29
25	**Test Yourself**	34
26	**Language Learning Diary**	34

Vocabulary Review: Educational Strategies

Faina Belkina emigrated from Russia. At school she reads, works on grammar and the dictionary, and practices conversation. At home Faina does homework, reads, and watches TV. Sometimes she talks with her neighbors.

What strategies do you use to learn English outside of class? Using the list and your own ideas, write what you do and **why** these methods are effective for you.

____

____

____

____

____

____

____

____

____

____

____

____

____

____

- speak with:
  - friends
  - coworkers
  - businesses
  - doctors, etc.
- ask for clarification
- call information numbers
- listen to the radio:
  - news
  - music
  - "talk" shows
- watch TV
- read the newspaper
- read magazines and books
- write in a journal
- make a vocabulary notebook
- use the dictionary for:
  - definitions
  - pronunciation
  - word formation
  - history
- use the library
- use computers:
  - to write
  - to study grammar
  - to use the Internet
- join community groups
- visit local points of interest

Study Skills and Strategies: Paraphrasing

Learning Strategy

Paraphrasing, or restating a text, helps you to make sure you understand the essential meaning. Taking the time to paraphrase helps you remember the main point and some details of the text.

Maria Munoz has been studying English through the Corpus Christi (Texas) Literacy Council since 1991. She studies at Del Mar Community College.

Read what Maria Munoz says about her education. Then paraphrase using clear, simple sentences. You may find it helpful to cover Maria's paragraph while you write.

I learned how to read and write just by writing what was in the computers. Then I started hearing the teachers say this and that and that's where I learned. I came here in 1991, and I sat down for a whole year at the computers by myself because the teachers thought I knew how to speak English. So I sat there and just looked at the pictures, and I started writing. Then, a teacher gave me a book to learn how to write my letters. We never finish learning because there is always something to learn. I am just going to keep on practicing to see where I can go. My main goal is to keep on so I can get my GED. Even though I don't have a car, I want to get my driver's license.

Grammar Review: Past Perfect Continuous

Michael **had been living** in Harrisburg for 10 years before he began to teach at Catholic Charities. Izrail **had been working** as an electrical engineer for 47 years before he left Russia. Adriana **had been working and studying** for several years before she moved to Pennsylvania.
Use the past perfect continuous tense to show action that continued for some amount of time before another action in the past. Sentences or clauses that use this tense often tell "how long" an action occurred in the past.

A. Use the following base forms of verbs + **had** + **been** + **ing** and a prepositional phrase that tells "how long" to practice the past perfect continuous.

Verbs	Prepositional Phrases
study	for three hours
speak	for many years
review	since 1992
listen	for about six months
learn	for half an hour
write	for two days

Fill in the blanks to make good sentences.

Example:

I ___had been listening___ to the radio ___for half an hour___ before I went to bed.

1. My friend ______________ English ______________ before she came to the United States.
2. Some students in the class ______________ English fluently ______________ before they began to study in class.
3. Because the woman was a good student, she ______________ her notes ______________ before the examination.
4. One man said that he ______________ English ______________.
5. When I called my friend, he said that he ______________ in his journal ______________.

B. Using the past perfect continuous, write about your study of English.

____

____

____

Doing It in English: Expressing Need

"I have to understand."

"I need to do something with my brain."

Learning Strategy

Because language use changes according to the situation, you need to know how to say the same idea in more than one way.

I need a job.
I need to work.
I have to study.
I must practice every day.
I've got to speak more.
It's necessary to listen carefully.

A. Sometimes the idea of **need** is expressed strongly as an obligation with words such as *have to* and *must.* (Example: *I have to go to the doctor this afternoon*). Write three sentences that express obligation.

____

____

____

B. Sometimes the idea of **need** expresses an idea of a wish or desire. (Example: *I need to get more exercise.*) Write three sentences that express desire.

____

____

____

Grammar Review: Using Base Words and Affixes

Reading Strategy
Look at the base word, the prefix, and the suffix to understand the meaning of a word and its function in a sentence.

Prefixes
un + happy = unhappy **re + try = retry**
A prefix is a letter or letters added to the beginning of a word that changes its meaning.

Suffixes
good + ness = goodness **help + ful = helpful**
A suffix is a letter or letters added to the end of a word to form a new word, particularly by changing the function of the word or its **part of speech.**

Base Words	Prefixes	Suffixes
accelerate	**bi-**	**-al/-able/-ible**
agree	**co-/com-/con-**	**-ate**
book	**de-**	**-er/-or**
comic	**dis-**	**-ful**
divide	**in-**	**-ish**
embark	**inter-**	**-ical**
employ	**intra-**	**-ly**
engage	**post-**	**-ment**
hostile	**pro-**	**-ness**
introduce	**re-**	**-ous**
try	**un-**	**-tion**
type		**-y-/-ity**
work		

Note: Sometimes the spelling changes. Example: happy + ness = happiness

Use the lists to make as many new words as possible. You can use your dictionary to help you understand the meanings and functions of the words.

______________________ ______________________

______________________ ______________________

______________________ ______________________

______________________ ______________________

______________________ ______________________

______________________ ______________________

Study Skills and Strategies: Using Context to Guess Meanings

Thu Thao Nguyen lives in Reston, VA. She studies computers at Northern Virginia Community College.

Reading Strategy

When you encounter an unfamiliar word in a reading, try to understand it by relating it to surrounding words and concepts that you do understand.

A. As you read the following article, try to understand unfamilar vocabulary in the context in which it is written. Even if a couple of the words are not clear, can you understand the main idea and main details of the article?

> In the old days, kids were in awe of their teachers, counselors, and other authority figures in school. The teachers sometimes seemed imposing and distant. In each school there was at least one teacher who seemed especially authoritarian and remote. One of the ways that these authority figures maintained order in school was by the tyranny of the "paddle." The paddle was a flat piece of wood, maybe 1½ feet long and ½ inch thick, designed to be easily gripped by the teacher as he applied it to the hindquarters of troublesome students. Luckily for the kids, there always were teachers in school who believed in teaching by patience, positive reinforcement, and kindliness.

B. List words or phrases that were unfamilar to you, your guess at their meanings, and how you arrived at that guess.

Words/Phrases	Meaning	Method of Understanding
authority figure	a person who has power	by reading words I know, like teacher, counselor—by joining the meaning of the two words: authority and figure

Vocabulary Review: Figures of Speech

Similes
Learning English is like making vegetable soup.
Similes compare two unlike things using the words **like** or **as.**

Metaphors
My first teacher was an angel.
A metaphor is a word or phrase used to stand for something different than its usual meaning.

A. In the following examples, write **S** before the phrase if it contains a simile and write **M** before the phrase if it contains a metaphor.

1. ______ He is smart like a fox.

2. ______ My boss is a real workhorse.

3. ______ Some people say that the United States is a melting pot.

4. ______ Other people say that the United States is like a patchwork quilt.

5. ______ He is a thief; he stole my heart.

6. ______ Throughout my illness, my brother has been a rock.

7. ______ In her new clothes, my daughter is just like a spring flower.

8. ______ English grammar is a puzzle to me.

B. Write similes or metaphors to express your feelings about the following persons, places, or things. Use the figures of speech within complete sentences.

your native country: ______________________________

____

____

the United States: ______________________________

____

____

your favorite teacher: ______________________________

____

____

More Reading and Writing: More Learning Strategies from Harrisburg

Adriana Ariza studies in a multilevel ESL class in Harrisburg.

Adriana:

Now, I live in Hummelstown because my husband has a fellowship at Hershey Medical Center in oncology and hematology. I need to speak English because I would like to work in microbiology. I studied in Colombia but, I can't work now because I don't speak English. I read English, but it is difficult for me to speak. In one year, I want to speak fluently. I study here five days a week from 9:00 to 12:00. After that I hope to work in my profession. First, probably, I would like to continue my studies to get a Masters' degree in microbiology. For me, it is easy to listen and to write. I listen to TV and radio. My frustration is that I can't speak with people. I get scared. My husband's partners are very nice because they speak slowly for me.

Arkady Mantaz studies at one of the classes run by Immigration and Refugee Services of Catholic Services. He was an electrician in the former Soviet Union for 31 years.

Arkady:

I began to study English a year before I came. It wasn't exactly studying. My brother left his books and notes when he came here in 1979 and I just used them. I like to read English books to compare English with German, which is my second language. It was okay to learn German because I was young, but now I have some problems because English is a very difficult language. Before I came here, the Russian scientists told us that the Russian language is the richest language. If you compare now, I feel that English is much richer—one meaning has a lot of words. I would like to read all English books without difficulty. Now, it's difficult for me only when I read some adjectives—not nouns, not verbs—because there are a lot of adjectives in the English language. I translate English books into Russian because I like this kind of activity.

Whose story, Adriana's or Arkady's, seems more like *your* story of learning English? Write a paragraph that expresses some of the challenges you face in learning English.

____

____

____

____

____

____

Doing It in English: Using Media for Focused Listening

Learning Strategy

When you listen to the radio or watch TV, videos, or movies, concentrate on understanding main ideas. When you listen again, try to listen for specific vocabulary and pronunciation.

A. Make a list of the kinds of listening you do outside of class. Then, put them in order with #1 being your favorite type.

____

____

____

____

____

____

____

B. You can develop a strategy for watching TV or movies by analyzing your own listening and watching. For the next week, take notes while you watch TV and try to discover some answers to the following questions:

1. When you watch something on TV (for example: the nightly news) what parts are easy for you to understand and what parts are more difficult?
2. Are the commercials easier to understand than the programs themselves? Why or why not?
3. How does the visual part of the program help you understand what you hear?
4. How often do you need to hear something repeated before you feel comfortable?
5. How much does dialect or accent affect your understanding?
6. Does your own level of knowledge and interest seem to affect your ability to understand? In what ways?

Test Yourself

Circle or fill in the correct answers.

1. Faina Belkina emigrated from Russia where she ________________ as a neurologist for 40 years.

   a) is working　　b) had been working　　c) was worked

2. Maria Munoz ________________ the computer for one year before she worked in a class.

   a) was using　　b) is using　　c) had been using

3. Ali Al-Shermery said, "I ________________ understand."

   a) must to　　b) got to　　c) have to

4. ________________ can be added to base words to change the function of the word.

   a) suffixes　　b) prefixes　　c) parts of speech

5. When ________________ are added to the beginning of a word, the meaning of the word changes.

   a) base words　　b) prefixes　　c) suffixes

6. He is smart ________________ a fox.

   a) like　　b) as　　c) such as

7. ________________ compare two unlike things using **like** or **as.**

   a) prefixes　　b) metaphors　　c) similes

8. Adriana Ariza ________________ for several years before she left Colombia.

   a) would be studying　　b) had been studying and working　　c) is working

9. Sometimes Arkady Mantaz wants to learn more about ________________.

   a) adjectives　　b) nouns　　c) verbs

Language Learning Diary

A. Think of what you've learned about schools, teachers, learning strategies. Also, think about the English you have learned in this unit. Using some of the prompts in the box as guides, write about what you've learned and would like to learn.

I learned about . . .
I spoke English to . . .
I listened to . . .
I read about . . .
I wrote about . . .
The strategies I used are . . .
I want to learn more about . . .

B. New words and phrases I want to remember. Keep a record of when you see, hear, or use a new word or phrase from this unit outside the classroom.

Word/Phrase	I saw it . . .	I heard it . . .	I used it . . .
metaphors	___________	on the radio	in a letter to my parents

Dating and Marriage in Washington, D.C.

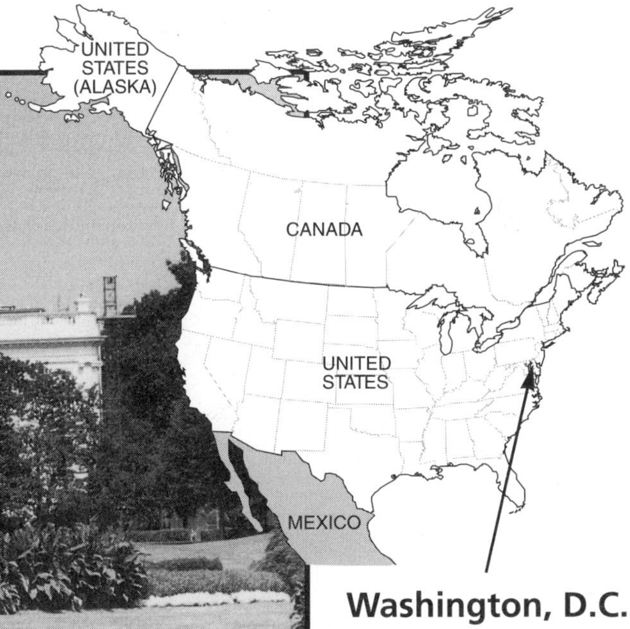

Washington, D.C.

When to Do Your Workbook Pages

Page		Do after Student Book Page
27	**Overview**	
28	**Study Skills and Strategies**	
	Inferring	37
29	**Vocabulary Review**	
	Using Phrasal Verbs	37
30	**Grammar Review**	
	Reported Speech	38
31	**More Reading and Writing**	
	Chet Kong's Story	39
32	**Vocabulary Review**	
	Describing Personal Characteristics	43
33	**Doing It in English**	
	Making and Responding to Invitations	44
34	**Doing It in English**	
	Reading a News Report	45
35	**Study Skills and Strategies**	
	Reading Graphs	45
36	**Grammar Review**	
	Parts of Speech	47
37	**Test Yourself**	50
38	**Language Learning Diary**	50

Study Skills and Strategies: Inferring

A. Read the conclusions about Sandeep and his parents. Find the sentences from the story in the text that suggest or infer each conclusion.

CONCLUSION	TEXT
1. Sandeep's parents taught their children their beliefs.	They instilled in us their values on dating and marriage.
2. Sandeep was stubborn.	______________________
3. Sandeep didn't date for two years.	______________________

Learning Strategy

To infer means to come to a conclusion based on information you have.

B. Read the following excerpts from Sandeep's story and answer the questions.

1. *My oldest sister was never allowed to go out on dates. . . . My other sister wanted to go out on dates and my parents tried to be a little more open with her.*
   What can you infer about Sandeep's parents?

   Sandeep's parents could be flexible.

2. *It was horrible because we didn't have a relationship for two years.*
   What can you infer about Sandeep?

   ____

3. *After two years they began to give in a little and I also gave in. They realized that for me and my friends dating did not mean marriage. During those two years they had a lot of opportunities to talk to their friends about what their kids were doing so they were slowly catching on to what dating meant here.*
   What can you infer about Sandeep's parents?

   ____

Vocabulary Review: Using Phrasal Verbs

Phrasal verbs are made by adding one or two prepositions after a verb. This changes the meaning of the verbs. Many phrasal verbs are idioms such as those in Sandeep's story.

A. Read Sandeep's story again on pages 36 and 37. Match these phrasal verbs from the story with the definitions.

1. grow up ______ **a.** to understand something

2. go out ______ **b.** to concede, to stop opposing someone, to quit

3. give in ______ **c.** to go someplace

4. catch on ______ **d.** to learn or discover something

5. come over __1__ **e.** to become an adult, to become mature

6. find out ______ **f.** to visit someone

B. Complete the sentences with the correct phrasal verb from the list above.

1. I ____grew up____ on a farm but after college I moved to the city.

2. Yesterday she ____________ a date with a man she met at her friend's party.

3. John needs to ____________ when the train will arrive so he won't be late.

4. After discussing it for a long time, Rachel's mother finally ____________ and let her go to Canada to visit her friend.

5. I'm finally ____________ to what these phrasal verbs mean.

6. He can't ____________ to my house to study because he has to take his daughter to the doctor.

C. Write your own sentences using the phrasal verbs from the story.

____

____

____

____

____

____

Grammar Review: Reported Speech

A. Read about Monisha's parents. What did her grandfather and her mother say to each other?

My parents' marriage was not arranged. My parents actually fought for eight years to get married. It was during the partition of India. My Dad's family had to come from Pakistan to India. They had to start their lives over from scratch.

My mother's family was very well off and my mother was the first daughter. My grandfather had been very liberal with her in many ways. She was the first woman in an all-male school and she was the first woman to become a lawyer in her state. But my grandfather did not want her to marry someone like my father.

"I have been open-minded, but I can go no further," he said. "You can not marry a poor refugee."

"Fine, but I will not marry anyone else," my mother told my grandfather. "I have my career," she said. "Marriage is not important to me so I will not get married."

My grandfather finally agreed to let her marry my father but it took eight years to work it out.

IDIOMS
from scratch
well off

B. Change the direct quotes to reported speech.

1. "I have been open-minded, but I can go no further."
   My grandfather said that he had been open-minded but he could go no further.
2. "You can not marry a poor refugee." ____________________
3. "I have my career." ____________________
4. "Fine, but I will not marry anyone else." ____________________
5. "Marriage is not important to me so I will not get married." ____________________

C. What are some things you remember your parents telling you about relationships. Write sentences using reported speech.

____

____

____

Reported Speech	
Quote He said, "I **need** to study English." She said, "I **wrote** a letter."	Reported Speech He said he **needed** to study English. She said that she **had written** a letter.
Reported speech tells what someone said without using a direct quote. **Direct quotes** in the simple past or present perfect can be changed to past perfect in reported speech.	

More Reading and Writing: Chet Kong's Story

A. Read about dating traditions in Cambodia. How do they compare to traditions in your country? Has Chet kept the traditions for his own daughter?

Dating is different in Cambodia than here. A boy and girl know each other for a long time before they start dating. They may have met at school or through a relative or friend and they make up their minds that they like each other before the first date. After they are sure of their feelings, a relative or a matchmaker arranges the first date. Once the boy *shows up* at the girl's house, he is committed. Once a couple starts dating, there is no way to *break up* because no other boy will want to marry that girl. For the boy it isn't too bad because he can *look for* another girl. However, it is considered a shame for the girl's family. Therefore, unless the boy really likes the girl, he doesn't want to start the dating process. That first date is like an arrow—there is only one direction to go.

In the United States people have a choice. If a relationship doesn't *work out,* they can break up and they can date someone else. But, they have to *watch out.* The choices they are facing are not always clear. My daughter lives here and grew up here so it is up to her who she dates. I can't make decisions for her. I can only tell her what I think is good or bad. I can tell her if I like someone or not, but she has to make up her own mind.

Chet Kong is a computer specialist. He works in Washington, D.C.

IDIOMS
up to her
make up her own mind

B. Find the *italicized* phrasal verbs in the story that mean the same as the verbs below.

arrive shows up

end a relationship ____________

search ____________

be careful ____________

to succeed ____________

C. Use three of the expressions in your own sentences.

1. ____________

2. ____________

3. ____________

Vocabulary Review: Describing Personal Characteristics

"A person should be patient and have a good sense of humor."

A. There are many ways to describe a person. We can describe a person's physical appearance, personality, or other general factors like the type of job a person has. Look at the list of words and phrases and arrange them into the three categories.

handsome	trustworthy	patient
educated	beautiful	is a good cook
tall	has a sense of humor	has a good job
rich	religion	attractive
flexible	is from my culture	kind

Physical Appearance	**Personality**	**Other**
handsome		

B. Write a paragraph describing someone you know. Include characteristics from the three categories—physical, personality, and other.

Doing It in English: Making and Responding to Invitations

Written invitations have many phrases that are important to know because they tell you what you should do or how you should respond.

A. Match the words and phrases below with the correct definition.

1. R.S.V.P.	______	informal party where food is cooked and eaten outdoors
2. Potluck	___1___	from the French (respondez s'il vous plait) which means please let the host know if you can attend
3. B.Y.O.B.	______	party for high school juniors and seniors, usually formal
4. Regrets only	______	you can wear informal, comfortable clothing
5. Surprise party	______	a dinner party where everyone brings food to share
6. Cookout	______	tuxedo and fancy dresses are required
7. Prom	______	the guest of honor does not know about the party
8. Bridal Shower or Baby Shower	______	you should bring something to drink: soda, beer, or wine
9. Black tie	______	you should wear a suit or nice dress
10. Formal	______	you should call the host only if you can not attend
11. Casual dress	______	a party to celebrate a wedding or birth in which a gift is expected

B. Read the invitation. Answer the questions. If not enough information is given, write a question mark.

PARTY
at Alicia's!

Time: 7:30 P.M.

When: Saturday, May 16

Where: 2345 Somerset Street

Regrets only at 538-2199

It's Pot Luck!

1. What time does the party begin? ______________________________.

2. Should I bring something to eat? ______________________________.

3. What should I wear to the party? ______________________________.

Doing It in English: Reading a News Report

A. The article below is about the changing trends in American marriages. What is the main idea and some of the important details the author includes in her report?

Americans Delay Trip to the Altar

Adapted from an article by Barbara Vobejda, Washington Post, 3/13/96

The Census Bureau reported yesterday that Americans are waiting longer to get married than at any time since the government started collecting statistics more than a century ago.

The median (average) age of first marriage—26.7 for men and 24.5 for women—has risen rapidly in recent years, reflecting a society of young people living quite differently than previous generations.

Instead of marrying shortly after high school, Americans now are more likely to attend college, live on their own, or move in with a partner for several years.

And those patterns have emerged because of a powerful combination of forces: economic changes that make it harder for young people to support themselves with just a high school degree, financial independence among working women, and increased social acceptance of unmarried couples living together.

In the early 1960s the median age for men getting married was about 22 and for women, about 20. This means that about half the brides were teenagers. Now, society generally views teenage girls as too young to marry.

Studies show that couples who marry earlier are more likely to divorce. Also women have more career opportunities open to them, giving them a psychological and financial independence most of their predecessors did not know.

But at the same time, the longer young people wait to marry, the more likely they are to conceive a child out of wedlock, demographers said. And studies have shown that children born to an unmarried mother are more likely to live in poverty and experience problems in school and elsewhere.

B. Check the best answers.

1. The main idea of this article is

- ❑ many young Americans are living together without getting married.
- ❑ teenage girls are too young to marry.
- ❑ more Americans are waiting longer to get married.

2. Which is <u>not</u> an important detail supporting the main idea?

- ❑ The Census Bureau started collecting statistics more than a 100 years ago.
- ❑ Economic changes make it harder for people to support themselves with only a high school degree.
- ❑ Society is more accepting of couples living together.

C. What do you think? Is this trend good or bad? State your reasons for your opinion.

____

____

____

Study Skills and Strategies: Reading Graphs

A. Look at the graph below. It reflects the information from the Census Bureau report on American marriage trends. Does this graph help to clarify ideas in the news report?

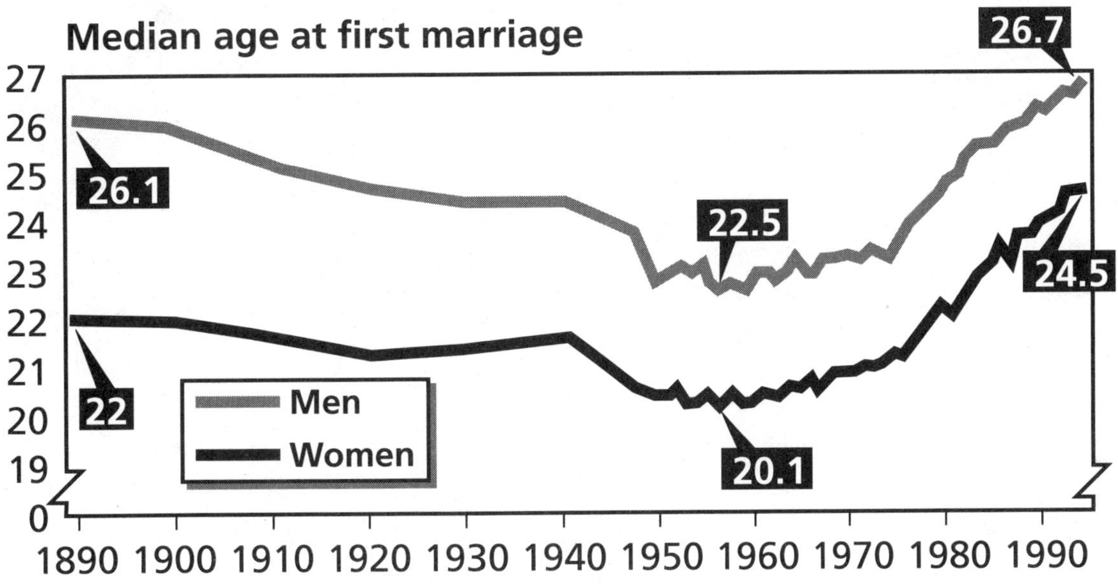

B. Circle the correct answer.

1. What is the topic of this graph? ______________________________

2. What period of time does this graph cover? ______________________________

3. What statement is not true?

- ❑ Between 1890 and 1900 the median age for women marrying was 22.
- ❑ Between 1890 and 1990 women married earlier than men.
- ❑ In 1940 men were marrying at an earlier age than in 1960.

4. This graph does not tell about

- ❑ the age men and women got married for the first time.
- ❑ why the age of the first marriage has changed.
- ❑ how old men and women are when they get married.

> **Learning Strategy**
>
> Line graphs show how things change over time. These changes are called **trends.** The period of time is usually shown on the horizontal ↔ scale. The vertical ↕ scale relates to the topic of the graph.

Grammar Review: Parts of Speech

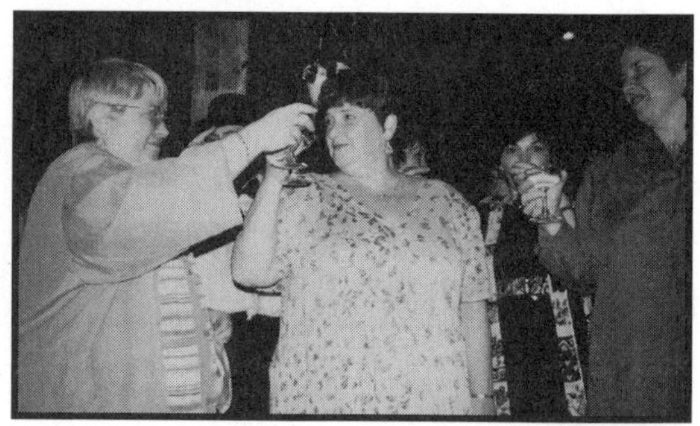

A. Read about the history of Valentine's Day.
Circle the verbs, underline the nouns, and write "A" over the adjectives.

February 14, also known as Valentine's Day, is a special day to celebrate love. It is a very old custom and many believe it dates back to the Roman Empire. The Romans had a celebration on February 15 called Lupercalia. On this day, young girls would put their names in a box. A young man would take out a name from the box to find his girlfriend for the next year. In other legends it is told that on February 14 birds choose their mates.

February 14 is also a day in the Catholic Church that honors several saints named Valentine. No one is sure if there is any relationship to one of these Saint Valentines and this day of honoring lovers.

In the nineteenth century people began sending cards to each other on Valentine's Day. This is still a very popular custom today. In addition, people now give each other heart-shaped boxes of chocolates, flowers, or jewelry. It has also become a day to tell relatives and friends how much they are loved.

B. Do you have a special day in your country to honor people you love? Write a paragraph about your holiday. Identify the verbs, nouns, and adjectives in your sentences.

____

____

____

____

____

____

____

Test Yourself

Circle or fill in the correct answers.

1. Would you like to go to lunch tomorrow?

a) I'm afraid. b) I'm sorry, I can't. c) I'd love.

2. He said that he ________________ to marry her.

a) wanted b) is wanting c) want

3. Would you be interested in ________________.

a) go to a movie? b) going to a movie? c) to go to a movie?

4. He ought to ________________ until he is older to start dating.

a) waiting b) waits c) wait

5. We don't let our daughter ________________ dates yet.

a) go out on b) go out in c) go out of

6. Which statement means the same thing? *She says that she needs to study.*

a) "I needed to study." b) "I need to study." c) "She needs to study."

7. I would like ________________ of milk in my coffee.

a) a little b) little bit c) a little bit

8. Do you want to eat out tonight?

a) I'd love to but, I can. b) I'd like that. c) Maybe some other times.

Language Learning Diary

A. Think about the ways individuals keep and change their marriage and dating customs in a new country **and** about the English you have learned in this unit. Using some of the prompts in the box as guides, write about what you have learned and would like to learn.

I learned about . . .
I spoke English to . . .
I listened to . . .
I read about . . .
I wrote about . . .
The strategies I used are . . .
I want to learn more about . . .

____

____

____

____

____

____

____

____

____

B. New words and phrases I want to remember. Keep a record of when you see, hear, or use a new word or phrase from this unit outside the classroom.

Word/Phrase	I saw it . . .	I heard it . . .	I used it . . .
find out	____________	on TV	at work: I asked my boss a question

Finding Success in Corpus Christi, Texas

When to Do Your Workbook Pages

Page		Do after Student Book Page
39	**Overview**	
40	**Vocabulary Review**	
	Describing Work Skills	54
41	**Grammar Review**	
	Embedded Questions	54
42–43	**Study Skills and Strategies**	
	Writing a Personal Data Sheet	55
44–45	**Doing It in English**	
	Filling Out a Job Application	55
46–47	**More Reading and Writing**	
	More About Delilah Flores	57
48	**Vocabulary Review**	
	Job and Career Titles	61
49	**Grammar Review**	
	Subject-Verb Agreement	65
50	**Grammar Review**	
	Agreeing, Disagreeing, and Being Unsure	66
51	**Test Yourself**	68
52	**Language Learning Diary**	68

Vocabulary Review Describing Work Skills

A. Sharon McKay is a teacher of English as a second language to adults, but she has had many other kinds of jobs. Read what Sharon says about her work skills.

Sharon McKay lives on a houseboat on the Potomac River in Washington, D.C.

I have been teaching English as a second language for eleven years. I have a bachelor's degree in English literature and secondary education and a master's degree in linguistics and bilingual education. I am well-qualified for this job, but I have had many other jobs for which I was not as well-qualified. Sometimes, I got the job simply because I was friendly and had a positive attitude.

One of my first interesting positions was as a librarian. I've been a children's librarian and a bookmobile librarian. I drove a library van around to people who could not drive to the library. I read children's stories, and I recommended novels to adults. It felt important to help people read.

When I began teaching English to adults, it was exciting and challenging work, and it still is. That is the reason I have been working in this field for so long. I may take other jobs, but I will always teach at least part of the time.

My many employment experiences have taught me a lot about myself and the interview process. You have to "blow your own horn" when you go to the interview. The employers only know what you tell them about yourself. I tell them I am flexible, cooperative, and diligent. I point to my employment history and show them how much I like working with people. I bring a boatload of enthusiasm to each interview and impress the employers with my high energy. I show them that I'm creative with my music and poetry as well. I try to present a real person in the interview, and I have had great success with this approach. For one job, I was hired over seventy-two other applicants! I must be doing something right.

IDIOMS
blow your own horn
boatload

B. Make a list of the words and phrases that Sharon used to describe her work skills.

______________________ ______________________

______________________ ______________________

______________________ ______________________

C. Make a list of words and phrases that describe your work skills.
Use words from Sharon's story, the box, or from your own knowledge.

____

____

____

____

____

self-motivated	energetic
independent	enthusiastic
hard-working	careful
loyal	eager
punctual	conscientious

Grammar Review: Embedded Questions

Embedded Questions
I asked Delilah if she liked her new job. Can you tell me if this job requires overtime work? Could you tell me whether experience is necessary for this job? Do you know who the supervisor is? I have no idea why I was transferred to the night shift.
Embedded questions are formed within other sentences. Indirect questions are embedded questions that retell a person's words. Embedded questions can also be polite ways to ask for information. Use **whether, if,** or **wh- questions** to begin embedded questions. Some, but not all, embedded questions require a question mark.

A. Interview your classmates. Write down some of your interview questions using indirect questions. Then, briefly write the answer you received.

Example:

Indirect Question: I asked whether Jalal worked when he was a student.
Answer: Jalal said he had worked part-time at the library.

1. **Indirect Question:** ______________________________

   Answer: ______________________________

2. **Indirect Question:** ______________________________

   Answer: ______________________________

3. **Indirect Question:** ______________________________

   Answer: ______________________________

B. Make a list of embedded questions that you could use to ask polite questions about a job opportunity.

Example:

I wonder if you could tell me if this job has health benefits.

____

____

____

____

____

Learning Strategy

Even before you begin a job search, you should gather important information about yourself. This should include personal statistics, job history, education, community and volunteer information.

Fill out the form below. Keep it handy when you are arranging interviews, writing a résumé for a job, or filling out an application.

Complete address ______________________________

____

Telephone numbers (home) ____________________

(work) ____________________

List all education including short courses, English study, and technical school. Remember dates, addresses, course of study, grade point average,* honors, and degrees. List the most recent and advanced study first.

*grade point average, or GPA, is your average overall grade, numerically expressed, with 4.0 as perfect

Education ______________________________

____

____

____

____

____

____

____

____

For employment history, list not only job titles, dates of employment, employers' names and addresses, but also skills required for the job, supervisors' names and titles, and beginning and ending salaries. The salary information is not always required information, and it should not be offered independently. Remember to include promotions and honors. List the current or more recent job first.

Employment ______________________________

____

____

____

____

____

____

____

____

Military Service ______________________________

____

Languages (other than English) ______________________________

Because a person can learn and use many skills outside of work, some employers want to know about community and volunteer activities. These activities should include church and charity activities. Mention what skills you've used such as organizing or fund-raising.

Community and Volunteer Service ______________________________

____

____

On an application, you may be asked whether you need special accommodations for a disability or if you have been convicted of a serious crime. Think of your answers in advance.

Other ______________________________

____

Doing It in English: Filling Out a Job Application

Often the information on the application is the first thing a boss or personnel manager knows about you. By filling out the application carefully, neatly, and fully, a prospective boss can begin to think well of you even before an interview.

Fill out the application.

Bill's Place
Homestyle Food

Application for Employment

An Equal Opportunity Employer

(Please type or print in black ink)

PERSONAL INFORMATION **Date** ____________________

Name: ____
Last First Middle

Address: ____
Number Street Apt.

____
City State Zip

Phone: (______) ____________________

EMPLOYMENT INFORMATION

Are you 18 years of age or over? **YES** ____ **NO** ____

Are you a U.S. citizen or legally eligible for employment in the U.S.? **YES** ____ **NO** ____

Social Security Number ______________________________

Position Applied for ____________________________ Salary Desired ______________

Are you able to perform this job (with or without accommodations)? **YES** ____ **NO** ____

Have you ever been convicted of a felony? **YES** ____ **NO** ____

If yes, please explain ____

Are you interested in **part-time** or **full-time** work? ______________________________

Circle the days you are able to work:

Sunday Monday Tuesday Wednesday Thursday Friday Saturday

Circle shifts you would be willing to work:

5:00 A.M.–1:00 P.M. 7:00 A.M.–3:00 P.M. 12:30 P.M.–9:00 P.M. 9:00 P.M.–5:00 A.M.

EDUCATION

Type of Institution	Name and Address	Dates Attended From	To	Graduated Yes/No	Degree/Diploma
High School	______________	______	______	______	______
	______________				
College or University	______________	______	______	______	______
	______________				
Technical	______________	______	______	______	______
	______________				
Other	______________	______	______	______	______
	______________				

What languages do you speak? ____________________________

EMPLOYMENT HISTORY

List your job history, starting with your most recent job.

Name/Address/Phone of Employer	Dates From	To	Position	Duties	Salary

I authorize Bill's Place to request relevant information from the schools and employers listed above. All information included in this application is true to the best of my knowledge.

Signature ______________________________ Date ______________

More Reading and Writing: More About Delilah Flores

Delilah Flores studied in a workplace class and an adult school funded through special Federal programs before she began attending NOVA (Northern Virginia Community College). She passed the National Teachers Exam so she could teach in the United States.

Since last September I have been teaching English as a second language to children at the Meyer Elementary School in Washington, D.C. This is the first time I have worked with young children because when I was in Venezuela I taught teenagers. The children I teach are from five to eight years old. Most of the children are from El Salvador, but some are from Vietnam, Nigeria, and other places in Africa. I thoroughly enjoy teaching these children. They like to pay attention, and they like me. It's wonderful.

I get to the school at eight-thirty and I teach until three-thirty. I usually stay at school until five-thirty or six o'clock. That's when I prepare my lessons. I teach about 120 students every day. I go into each classroom and work with the children in the class while the classroom teacher is working with the rest of the class. Each of the classes is about forty-five minutes long. I do a lot of planning for my classes, and I have to adapt the plans for different children. Each class I teach is multilevel because in each class there are children at different levels of English.

One thing I don't like is playground duty. I have to watch the kids during recess for half an hour every other day. I don't like watching all the kids because sometimes the kids are rough, and I don't always know how to control them. There are a lot of accidents, and sometimes, I have to intevene when children are having a fight.

There's another thing that worries me about my job. I have to take the metro and the bus to get home to Alexandria (VA). When I stay late at school, I feel very nervous about walking to the metro in the dark. It is not a safe neighborhood. I have applied to teach in Fairfax County (VA), so I may be able to teach there.

When I worked at the microfilm lab, I found my job boring and repetitive. Now, I'm much happier because I use my brain. I still have my long-term goal of attaining my master's degree in biochemistry, but now I also have a different idea. Instead, I think I might want to get a master's degree in bilingual education.

My advice to other people is to keep working toward their goals and to keep learning English. I have really learned to appreciate the classes I took at REEP (Arlington Education and Employment Program). I was encouraged to reach my goals. My first teacher was Sharon McKay. She taught an English class at my workplace, Gates-Hudson, a building maintenance company. Sharon encouraged me to study more at school. I waited about a month, and then I went to class. This has made a big difference in my life.

A. Reread both stories about Delilah. Summarize her work history. Remember, a summary should contain the main ideas and important details. A summary should also be short and objective.

____

B. Now, summarize your own work history in your native country or in the United States.

____

C. What advice can you give other students?

____

Vocabulary Review: Job and Career Titles

Reading Strategy

Learn the specialized vocabulary of your job or hobby. Learn what the words mean, how to spell them, and how to pronounce them. Use the dictionary, a book on the subject, or ask an expert.

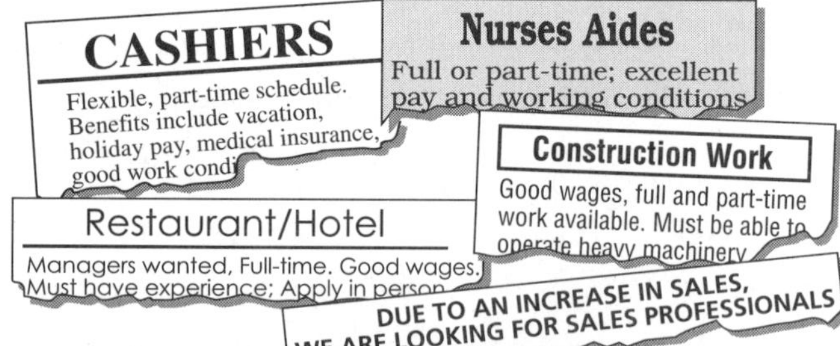

A. Knowing job titles and job-related vocabulary helps you understand the Help Wanted section of the newspaper, speak confidently in interviews, and fill out applications properly. Use the clues to complete the puzzle.

Across:

1. provides construction work for a fee
3. man or woman who waits on you at restaurant
5. fixes the wiring in a house
7. uses a brush inside or outside
9. files in the office
11. they tell the computers what to do
13. physicians
15. gives you a lift from the airport
16. cleans at the hotel
17. operates machines, systems, or trains

Down:

1. takes money, gives change
2. has compassion, gives shots
4. growing food is the business
6. represents clients in court
8. you are the learner, they are the ________
10. this person slices, chops, and sautes
12. this person keeps the financial records
14. Mariano Ramos Hernandez

Grammar Review: Subject-Verb Agreement

Subject-Verb Agreement
The man <u>looks</u> at the job application. I <u>have</u> a new supervisor. Delilah <u>has</u> a new job. Thu-Thuy and her brother <u>study</u> at NOVA. The class <u>is</u> working on a project together.
The subject noun or pronoun must agree in number and person with its verb. A collective noun usually takes a singular verb.

Person in English		
	Singular	Plural
First person:	I have	We have
Second person:	You have	You have
Third person:	She/He/It has	They have

A. Tom Terrill works for the U.S. Department of Labor. As you read the paragraph about Tom's work, circle the correct verb form.

I (work, works) for the Office of Workers Compensation Programs. I (have, has) an office on Constitution Avenue in Washington, D.C., but I (work, works) at home four days a week. Some of my office friends (don't like, doesn't like) working at home, but I (finds, find) myself liking it a lot. Federal employees (tell, tells) me about their work-related injuries, and I (decide, decided) if they (should get, should gets) any compensation. Hearings officers like me (travel, travels) around the country to listen to federal employees' claims. The federal workforce (need, needs) workers' compensation. Congress (is, are) in charge of the funds for my program.

B. Write four sentences about jobs you've had. Practice using subjects in different persons and numbers.

First Person Singular: ______________________________

____

First Person Plural: ______________________________

____

Third Person Singular: ______________________________

____

Third Person Plural: ______________________________

____

Grammar Review: Agreeing, Disagreeing, and Being Unsure

Agreeing, Disagreeing, and Being Unsure		
Agree:	**Disagree:**	**Unsure:**
I agree with you (or with that idea).	I don't agree.	I can't decide.
I think that's true.	I'm not sure I can agreewith that idea.	I'm just not sure.
I think that's right.	I can't agree with that completely.	I think I need some more time to think about this issue.
You've expressed my idea perfectly.	I'm afraid we are not in agreement.	

There are many ways to express the degree to which you agree, disagree, or remain unsure about a statement or idea. The words you choose can express how strong you feel. Read these statements about English and write a comment that shows the strength of your opinion about it.

1. English should be the official language of the United States. People shouldn't live here if they don't want to learn English.

____

____

2. Reading American novels that contain dialects and slang helps a person to learn "real" English.

____

____

3. Teachers who weren't born in the United States can't help immigrants learn English. They have to fix their own accents first!

____

____

4. Americans shouldn't talk so fast. Immigrants can't understand them. Don't they want us to learn English?

____

____

Test Yourself

Circle or fill in the correct answers.

1. Sharon McKay says she is ______________________, cooperative, and diligent.

   a) flustered b) frightened c) flexible

2. Indirect questions are ______________________.

   a) embedded questions b) part of the past perfect c) in quotation marks

3. Do you know ______________________ Sharon likes teaching?

   a) weather b) whether c) while

4. You should write your personal data sheet ______________________ you fill in a job application.

   a) before b) at the same time c) after a job interview

5. Delilah Flores ______________________ enjoys teaching elementary school children.

   a) throughly b) thorough c) thoroughly

6. Delilah ______________________ playground duty because sometimes the kids are rough.

   a) don't like b) whether she liked c) doesn't like

7. The class ______________________ embedded questions.

   a) are studying b) is studying c) have studying

8. Tom Terrill and his co-workers ______________________ an office in Washington D.C.

   a) work b) have c) has

9. "English should be the official language," is a(n) ______________________.

   a) embedded question b) opinion c) law

Language Learning Diary

A. Think about ways you've learned to describe your jobs and job skills, to look for jobs, **and** about the English you've learned in this unit. Using some of the prompts in the box as guides, write about what you've learned and would like to learn.

I learned about . . .
I spoke English to . . .
I listened to . . .
I read about . . .
I wrote about . . .
The strategies I used are . . .
I want to learn more about . . .

____

____

____

____

____

____

____

____

____

B. New words and phrases I want to remember. Keep a record of when you see, hear, or use a new word or phrase from this unit outside the classroom.

Word/Phrase	I saw it . . .	I heard it . . .	I used it . . .
conscientious	newspaper	__________	with my boss

Special Communities
Refugees in Comer and Atlanta, Georgia

When to Do Your Workbook Pages

Page		Do after Student Book Page
53	**Overview**	
54	**Grammar Review**	
	Writing Wh- Questions	72
55	**Vocabulary Review**	
	Describing Places	72
56	**More Reading and Writing**	
	Nermina Silnovic's Story	73
57	**Grammar Review**	
	Asking for Help	74
58–59	**Doing It in English**	
	Opening a Bank Account	74

Page		Do after Student Book Page
60	**Doing It in English**	
	Filling out Health Forms	74
61	**Study Skills and Strategies**	
	Reading Tables	76
62–63	**Study Skills and Strategies**	
	Using Transition Words	79
64	**Study Skills and Strategies**	
	Outlining a Speech to Inform	80
65	**Test Yourself**	84
66	**Language Learning Diary**	84

Grammar Review: Writing Wh- Questions

A. The refugees spend a few months at the Jubilee community. What questions do you have about this community? Write them here.

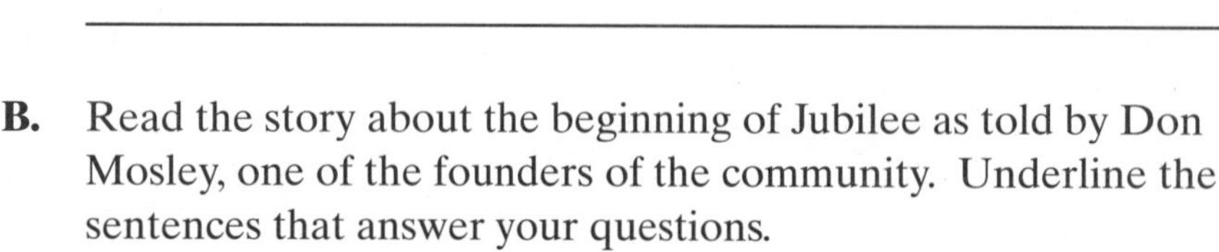

B. Read the story about the beginning of Jubilee as told by Don Mosley, one of the founders of the community. Underline the sentences that answer your questions.

Don Mosley is one of the founding partners of Jubilee.

Six adults and six children came to Comer, Georgia, to establish a new community of service in the spring and summer of 1979. The week that my family came, I saw the July 2, 1979 issue of Newsweek about the boat people of Vietnam. The front cover picture struck me even before I read the article. Then I read the article two times and when I got unpacked, I sat down and wrote a one page proposal for making Jubilee a refugee welcome center. Within two or three hours the other partners read it and became excited too. Out of that grew the refugee program at Jubilee. We have had almost 2,000 refugees come through Jubilee. The first were Cubans in 1980, followed by Laotian and Vietnamese families. There have been refugees from Cambodia, Afghanistan, Haiti, Bosnia, and many from Central America.

Jubilee's official goal is to give the refugees an introduction to spoken English. The other thing we do is to make them feel loved and secure in this new setting so that they have the best possible first step into their new life in this new culture.

IDIOM
struck me

C. Read the answers and write the questions.

1. ____________________? In Comer, Georgia.
2. ____________________? In the spring of 1979.
3. ____________________? He read an article in Newsweek .
4. ____________________? About 2,000 refugees.
5. ____________________? They were from Cuba.
6. ____________________? To give refugees an introduction to spoken English.
7. ____________________? To make them feel loved and secure.

Vocabulary Review: Describing Places

A. Many words in English have a noun and adjective form. Common adjective endings are: -y, -ed, -ous, -al, and -ful. Find the adjective for the noun in the box. Write it in the correct column. Use the dictionary if you need help.

hill	mountain	storm	fog	crowd
peace	wind	congestion	breeze	noise
excitement	cloud	relaxation	nature	pollution

-ed	-y	-ful	-ous	-al
crowded	hilly	______	______	______
______	______			
______	______			
______	______			
______	______			
	______			
	______			

B. Think about a special place you like to go when you want to relax or think. What words describe this place? List them here.

__________ __________ __________

__________ __________ __________

C. Write a brief description of your special place. Use nouns and adjectives to give a detailed description.

____

____

____

____

____

____

More Reading and Writing: Nermina Silnovic's Story

A. Read Nermina Silnovic's story. Underline examples that show how Nermina felt about Jubilee.

My family has been in the United States for about fifteen months. We arrived at Jubilee in December. I remember when we came to Jubilee we were a little shocked because we didn't expect to be living in a rural place. Our image of the United States from watching TV was different. However, we quickly began to feel comfortable and I can tell you that that period was the nicest period of my life here in the United States. Everything was okay there. It was so peaceful, we could finally relax.

We studied English there four hours every day except Sunday. We had good teachers. We knew we were only staying at Jubilee a short time. They prepared us for life in Atlanta. It was very helpful. For example, there was one volunteer who met with us to show us how to open a bank account. He came into class all dressed up like a professional and he was carrying a briefcase. He showed us how it would be at the bank. We practiced answering questions.

When I came to Atlanta I started going to school but I had to stop because only my father was working and we couldn't pay the rent or utilities on his income. Recently we had good news that my brother has escaped to Croatia from Bosnia and we are expecting him in a few months. Perhaps when my brother comes, he will start work and I will be able to go back to school.

Nermina Silnovic is from Bosnia. She came to Jubilee with her mother and father.

B. What is the main idea of each paragraph?

Paragraph 1 ______

Paragraph 2 ______

Paragraph 3 ______

C. What did you need to learn about your new community when you first arrived?

______

______

D. How did you get information about your community when you first arrived?

- ❑ a neighbor
- ❑ myself
- ❑ a friend or relative
- ❑ a teacher

Grammar Review: Asking for Help

Can you give me a hand?

Sure.

Would you show me how to hook up the VCR?

I'd be glad to.

Thanks.

Don't mention it.

A. Think about a situation in which you would ask someone for help. Write the conversation.

Speakers: ______________________

____

Relationship of speakers: ______________________

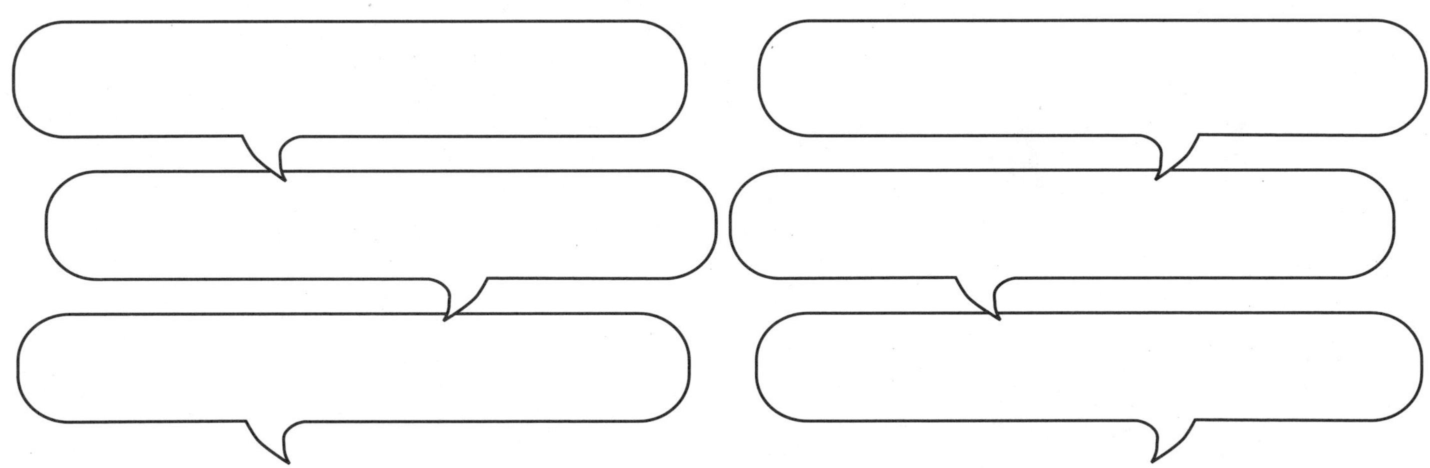

Requests with Would, Could, Can, and Will	
Would you please **Could** you please **Can** you **Will** you	open the door for me?
The verb that follows *would, could, can,* and *will* is in the simple form.	

Responding to Requests with *"Would you mind"*		
Request	**Can help**	**Can't help**
Would you mind driving me to school?	No, I wouldn't mind at all. No. I'd be happy to drive you.	Sorry, I can't because . . . I'd like to but I can't because . . .
To respond to a request for help using **would you mind,** answer "No" if you want to help. This means you don't mind or that it is not a problem for you.		

Doing It in English: Opening a Bank Account

A. Read the conversation between the bank officer and the customer.

I'd like to open a savings account.
How much would you like to deposit?
Is there a minimum?
Yes, there is a $250 minimum deposit.
Can I make withdrawals without a penalty?
Yes. You can make six withdrawals each quarter.
Do you mean six withdrawals every three months?
That's right.
I see. What do I need to do?
I need to see some identification and you need to answer a few questions for the application.

B. What other questions could the customer ask the bank officer?

____

____

____

____

C. Check (✔) the boxes appropriate for you.

- ☐ I have a savings account.
- ☐ I have a checking account.
- ☐ I want a savings account.
- ☐ I have an ATM card.
- ☐ I want a checking account.
- ☐ I save money every month.
- ☐ I pay for most things with cash.
- ☐ I pay for most things by check.

D. Complete the following. If I received $500 as a gift, I would

____

____

"There was one volunteer who met with us to show us how to open a bank account. We practiced answering questions. It was very helpful."

Scan the brochure on ATM safety and answer the questions.

ATM Safety

With ATMs (Automatic Teller Machines) you can get cash, make deposits and check your balance quickly and easily. Here are a few safety tips to keep your electronic banking safe and secure.

Your ATM card is like cash.
Keep your card in a safe place. Your personal identification number or PIN will only work with your card. Don't write your number on the card. It is best to memorize it.

Report a lost or stolen card immediately.
Even though the card can't be used without your PIN, it is best to quickly report the card stolen or lost.

Always observe the area around an ATM walk-up before leaving your car.
If you see anyone or anything strange or suspicious, don't get out of the car. Leave the area immediately. It's also a good idea not to go alone to a walk-up.

Stand in a position so that other people cannot see you enter your PIN or know how much you withdrew.

Have your card ready to use. Leave the area quickly when you are finished with your transactions.

1. What is an ATM?

____

____

2. What does PIN mean?

____

3. Why should you memorize your PIN?

____

4. If you lose your card, what should you do?

____

____

5. What can you do so no one will see you enter your PIN?

____

____

6. What other safety tips can you think of when using an ATM?

____

____

____

Doing It in English: Filling Out Health Forms

Fill out the form with your information.

PATIENT INFORMATION

Patient Name ______________________________ Date __________
Last First MI

❑ Male ❑ Female ❑ Married ❑ Single ❑ Child ❑ Other __________

Address ______________________________
Street

____
City State Zip Code

Phone (Home) __________ (Work) __________

Social Security # __________ Birth Date __________

HEALTH HISTORY

Have you had any of the following? Please check those that apply.

❑ AIDS
❑ Anemia
❑ Arthritis
❑ Asthma
❑ Cancer
❑ Diabetes
❑ Dizziness
❑ Epilepsy
❑ Fainting
❑ Glaucoma
❑ Head Injuries
❑ Heart Disease
❑ Hepatitis
❑ High Blood Pressure
❑ Pregnancy
❑ Sinus Problems
❑ Stomach Problems
❑ Stroke
❑ Tuberculosis
❑ Ulcers
❑ Venereal Disease

• Do you have any allergies? ❑ Yes ❑ No

If yes, please explain. ______________________________

• Have you had surgery? ❑ Yes ❑ No

If yes, please explain. ______________________________

• Do you smoke? ❑ Yes ❑ No

If yes, how much per day? __________.

INSURANCE INFORMATION

Name of Insured: ______________________________
Last First MI

Insured's Address: ______________________________
Street City State Zip Code

ID # __________ Group # __________ Insured's Birth Date: __________

Insurance Plan Name __________ Insurance Plan Address __________

To the best of my knowledge, all the above information is true.

______________________________ __________
Signature of patient, parent, or guardian Date

Study Skills and Strategies: Reading Tables

Persons Who Performed Unpaid Volunteer Work in the United States During the Year Ending May 1989
(numbers in thousands)

	Men			Women		
Characteristics	**Total number of men**	**Volunteer Workers**	**Percent of age group**	**Total number of women**	**Volunteer Workers**	**Percent of age group**
Total	88,729	16,681	18.8	97,539	21,361	21.9
Age						
16 to 24 years	15,912	1,814	11.4	16,427	2,152	13.1
25 to 34	21,138	3,678	17.4	21,748	5,002	23.0
35 to 44	17,474	4,683	26.8	18,301	5,655	30.9
45 to 54	11,931	2,601	21.8	12,734	3,069	24.1
55 to 64	10,035	1,987	19.8	11,321	2,468	21.8
65 years and older	12,133	1,917	15.8		3,016	17.7
Employment Status						
Employed	64,178	13,734	21.4	52,950	12,705	24.0
Unemployed	3,243	360	11.1	2,887	485	16.8
Not in labor force	21,205	2,587	12.2	41,689	8,171	19.6

Source: U.S. Department of Labor, Bureau of Labor and Statistics

Read the table and answer the questions.

1. What is the topic of this table? ______________________________
2. What is the subject of the first column? ______________________________

____
3. In general, who did more volunteer work? Men? Women? ______________________________
4. Which age group of men has the largest number of volunteers? ______________________________
5. What percent of unemployed women do volunteer work? ______________________________
6. What information from this table surprised you? Why? ______________________________

____

____

____

Study Skills and Strategies: Using Transition Words

Transition words help to connect one sentence to another. They make it easier to follow and understand what a writer says.

A. Study the chart of transition words.

Transition Word	Usage
first, second, then, finally	sequences ideas in chronological order or order of importance
and, in addition, moreover	adds an idea
but, however	shows contrast, adds an opposite idea
and, also	adds similar ideas
for example	gives an example
because, for, since	tells the reason or cause
so, therefore	tells the result, the effect, or consequence

B. Read Chou Ly's story. Underline the transition words.

I've been at Jubilee since 1982, first as a volunteer and then as a partner. Before that, I came here as a refugee from Cambodia. When I heard about living in a community like this I had no idea what it meant. I had mixed feelings and I was not sure I would like it here. The service to refugees, the working for peace and justice I liked, but the one thing that made me uncomfortable was the way of living. Here people live in separate houses but we share one common meal a day. Also we have a common kitchen to prepare that meal and a bell to ring when it's time to eat. It brought back memories of Cambodia under communism because there we had all common meals and bells ringing too. It took me a few years to get adjusted to it. When I began to understand more English, I understood what was going on and I felt better. I began to like it so I became a partner.

Chou Ly is the Refugee Host at Jubilee Partners. She is from Cambodia.

Now I am the refugee host, therefore, I really get to know the refugees. I visit with them when they are not in class or doing things. I try to make them feel comfortable here. Also I try to let them know people care about them. When they talk about being scared and confused because everyone is speaking English, I tell them about when I first arrived because I was just like them. When I look back I understand that God had a plan for me to survive and come here to serve other people who are in the same situation that I was in.

C. List the different roles, in chronological order, that Chou Ly has had at Jubilee.

1. ____________________

2. ____________________

3. ____________________

4. ____________________

D. Read the next passage by Chou Ly and choose the best transition word to complete the sentences.

I like the interactions with the refugees. I like learning a few words of their language, ____________________ *(but, moreover, finally),* they like teaching us their language. They feel like they are sharing something with us—their language, their culture, their food.

I remember one Salvadoran family. I felt very close to them. They had been through a lot of difficult times before they got to Jubilee ____________________ *(first, for example, but)* they were very strong people.

It didn't take long to get to know them ____________________ *(because, however, and)* they were very friendly. I was working in the clothing store at that time ____________________ *(for example, but, and)* I would open up early for them and fix the clothing that didn't fit them. When their departure was delayed for a few weeks they were so happy, and so was I, ____________________ *(therefore, for, next)* we had become friends.

Study Skills and Strategies: Outlining a Speech to Inform

Choose a country to talk about. Complete the outline for your speech.

Title: ______________________________.

Learning Strategy
An outline helps organize information for a speech. It is a useful guide that shows the introduction, the main points, and the conclusion.

Introduction:

____

____

____

I. Main idea:

A. Supporting details

1.

2.

II. Main idea:

A. Supporting details

1.

2.

III. Main idea:

A. Supporting details

1.

2.

Conclusion:

____

____

____

It is easier to write the introduction and conclusion after you have chosen the main ideas.

Test Yourself

Circle or fill in the correct answers.

1. Where do you ______________ go after class?

   a) would like b) want to c) must

2. Would you mind ______________ me to work tomorrow?

   a) driving b) drive c) to drive

3. Senita ______________ speak better English.

   a) must to b) have to c) has to

4. ______________ did you learn about your English class?

   a) What b) How c) Who

5. I like helping my friends ______________ to helping my family.

   a) but b) and c) in addition

6. The city was crowded and ______________.

   a) noise b) noisy c) pollution

7. The hills were covered with a dense ______________.

   a) stormy b) foggy c) fog

8. I want to study English ______________ I don't have time.

   a) because b) also c) but

Language Learning Diary

A. Think about about the ways communities help new arrivals **and** about the English you have learned in this unit. Using some of the prompts in the box as guides, write about what you've learned and would like to learn.

I learned about . . .
I spoke English to . . .
I listened to . . .
I read about . . .
I wrote about . . .
The strategies I used are . . .
I want to learn more about . . .

B. New words and phrases I want to remember. Keep a record of when you see, hear, or use a new word or phrase from this unit outside the classroom.

Word/Phrase	I saw it . . .	I heard it . . .	I used it . . .
give a hand	____________	on TV	I asked a co-worker for help

Staying in Touch

Stories from Laos and California

When to Do Your Workbook Pages

Page		Do after Student Book Page
67	**Overview**	
68	**Vocabulary Review**	
	Ways of Staying in Touch	86
69–70	**Doing It in English**	
	Sending International Mail	86
71–72	**Study Skills and Strategies**	
	Recognizing Levels of Formality in Writing	88
73	**Grammar Review**	
	Using Conditional Sentences	90
74	**Grammar Review**	
	Expressing Wishes	92
75	**Study Skills and Strategies**	
	Adding Factual Information	94
76	**Study Skills and Strategies**	
	Recognizing Time and Sequence Clues	96
77	**More Reading and Writing**	
	Native Country: Memories of Vietnam	98
78	**Vocabulary Review**	
	Major Life Events	99
79	**Test Yourself**	101
80	**Language Learning Diary**	101

Vocabulary Review: Ways of Staying in Touch

A. Members of the Dengvilay family who immigrated to America stay in touch with their parents in Laos by writing letters, sending photographs, and going back to Laos for occasional visits.

How do you stay in touch with friends and relatives back home? Check the means of communication you use to send and receive news. Add others to the list if you wish.

- ☐ letters
- ☐ telephone
- ☐ fax
- ☐ electronic mail (e-mail)
- ☐ photographs
- ☐ videotapes
- ☐ audiotapes
- ☐ post cards
- ☐ ______________________
- ☐ ______________________

B. Complete the following sentences.

1. My country of origin is ______________________.
2. The people I stay in touch with there are ______________________.
3. I communicate with them most often by ______________________.
4. They communicate with me by ______________________.
5. One day, I would like to ______________________.

Doing It in English: Sending International Mail

A. Read this message from the U.S. Postal Service. Then decide if the envelope at the bottom of the page is correctly addressed.

ADDRESSING INTERNATIONAL MAIL

Destination Address

The full address should be typed or legibly written in English and placed lengthwise on one side of the item. An address in a foreign language is permitted if the names of the city, province, and country are also indicated in English.

The last line of the address block area must show only the country name, written in full (no abbreviations) and in capital letters. Foreign postal codes (numeric or alpha), if used, should be placed on the line above the destination country as shown below.

Line 1: NAME OF ADDRESSEE
Line 2: STREET ADDRESS or POST OFFICE BOX NUMBER
Line 3: POSTAL CODE (if used), CITY, and PROVINCE or STATE
Line 4: COUNTRY NAME (uppercase letters in English)

Examples:

Jaques Molier	Ms. J. Meggs
Rue De Champaign	Apartado 3068
06570 St. Paul	46807 Puerto Vallarto
FRANCE	MEXICO

Sender's Return Address

The Sender's name and address, including ZIP Code and country of origin, should be shown on all mail. If a letter or parcel cannot be delivered, a return address ensures that the item is returned to the sender, if appropriate.

Is this letter addressed correctly? If not, circle the parts that are incorrect.

B. The U.S. Post Office classifies international mail into several categories, six of which are described in the chart below. Read the descriptions of each category, then identify the examples below the chart.

Type of Mail	Description
Letters and Letter Packages	All mail items that contain personal, handwritten, or typewritten, communications. Unless prohibited by the destination country, merchandise, or other items may also be mailed at the letter rate. The weight limit to all countries is four pounds.
Post Cards and Postal Cards	Post cards and postal cards are single cards sent without a wrapper or an envelope. Folded (double) cards must be sent in envelopes at the letter rate.
Aerogrammes	Aerogrames are air letter sheets that can be folded into the form of an envelope and sealed. Tape or stickers must not be used to seal aerogrammes. Enclosures are not permitted in aerogrammes.
Printed Matter	Printed matter means paper on which words, letters, characters, figures, images, or any combination of these has been printed (not handwritten or typed). This class includes newspapers, magazines, books, and sheet music. Items not acceptable as printed matter are certificates, photographs, slides, films, sound, or video recordings.
Small Packets	This class of mail is for gifts, merchandise, commercial samples, or documents that are not personal correspondence. This class is also used for sending audio- and videotapes of any kind.
Parcel Post	This class includes all merchandise or any other articles that are not required to be mailed at letter postage rates. For example, personal correspondence may not be included. Maximum weight limits for parcel post items vary from country to country, but they are usually 22 or 44 pounds.

Item	Category
1. a personal letter with photographs enclosed	______________________
2. a home video showing a child's birthday party	______________________
3. a hundred copies of a newspaper article	______________________
4. an electric hair dryer as a gift to a relative	______________________
5. a personal letter written on a special air letter sheet with no enclosures	______________________

Study Skills and Strategies: Recognizing Levels of Formality in Writing

A. Look at these five samples of different types of writing. Notice the differences in style.

After 1975, life became very hard for us here in Laos. That's why five of our children decided to leave. We worried about them night and day. We were really upset when we heard that our oldest daughter got robbed!

Sample A

Mom and Dad—
Will be at soccer practice until 5:30. Please pick me up, OK?
love,
Noi

Sample B

More than half of the population of Laos is made up of ethnic minorities living in the remote mountainous regions of the country. These groups include the Homing, Mien, Yao, and Khmu.

Sample C

Mr. and Mrs. Thongvangsy
and
Mr. and Mrs. Sylaphone
request the honor of your presence
at the marriage of their children
Noulek Thongvangsy
Samphan Sylaphone
on Saturday the nineteenth of June
nineteen hundred and ninety seven

Sample D

Dear Mrs. Sylaphone,

I am pleased to inform you that your application for admission to the continuing education program at Providence Community College has been approved. Please use the enclosed form to enroll for classes beginning on January 17. A schedule of fees is also included, along with an application for financial aid. If you have any questions, please do not hesitate to contact me directly.

Sample E

B. Match the samples above with the descriptions below. Write the sample letter of each style of writing next to its description .

______ Language is very formal, but not written in paragraph form. Dates and addresses are completely spelled out. Usually printed on a card or beautiful paper.

______ Very informal and often not written in complete sentences. Frequently used between close friends or family members. Usually handwritten.

______ Written in the first person (I, we) to tell about something that happened from a personal point of view.

______ Addressed to someone who is not a close friend of the writer. Titles (Mr., Mrs., Ms., Dr.) and last names are used to address the reader. Language is polite and formal.

______ Gives information about a topic to interested readers. Written in the third person (he, she, it, they) *about* a place, person, or thing.

C. Refer to this list to write the name of the writing style represented by each sample.

Sample A: personal narrative

Sample B: personal note

Sample C: descriptive essay

Sample D: formal invitation

Sample E: formal letter

D. Which writing style would you use in each of the following situations?

1. You came over to visit a close friend, but she is not home.

____

2. Your teacher has asked you to write several paragraphs about your country to inform other students and teachers in your school or program.

____

3. You are applying for a job by mail. You need to include a cover letter with your résumé.

____

4. You are keeping a personal journal or diary in English.

____

5. Your twenty-fifth wedding anniversary is coming up, and you are planning a big celebration.

____

E. Choose one of the situations above (or a very similar one) and write a sample of the writing style you would use. You can either write a short paragraph or a few lines of a formal invitation.

____

____

____

____

____

____

____

Grammar Review: Using Conditional Sentences

Saisana Dengvilay lives in Luang Prabang, Laos with his parents, his grandmother, and two older sisters. He graduated from secondary school last year. He speaks a little English, and he works in his family's store near the Mekong River. In this photo, he is in a boat crossing the Mekong for a family picnic at a Buddhist temple on the other side of the river.

A. Read the information under the photograph and imagine how Saisana's life would be different if he had left Laos ten years ago. Complete the sentences below with your own ideas. Remember that you can use conditional sentences to talk about past, present, or future possibilities.

Past: If I had stayed in my country, I **would have gotten married** much earlier.
Present: If we didn't have good jobs, we **might not stay** here long.
Future: If they became citizens of this country, they **could travel** more easily.

To form past conditionals, use a modal *(would, could, might)* + (not) have + the past participle form of the verb. To form present and future conditional sentences, use a modal + base form of the verb.

1. If he hadn't stayed in Laos, ______________________________.
2. If he lived in California, ______________________________.
3. If he decided to leave now, ______________________________.

B. How would your life be different if you had not come to live in this country? What do you think would (or would not) have happened? Write a paragraph of at least five sentences.

____

____

____

____

____

Grammar Review: Expressing Wishes

A. Fill in the missing words without referring to your student book.

First, I wish I ________________ go back home to visit my grandmother again. And I ________________ my children could come with me so they ________________ see where we are from. My third wish is one for the whole world—I wish there would never ________________ another war.

B. Think about things you wish you could change. Fill in the chart with notes that describe some of the current facts and wishes in your life. List as many ideas as you can.

	Fact	**Wish**
myself	rent an apartment	own a house
my family		
my community		
my country		
the world		

C. Based on the information in your chart, write five sentences explaining your wishes.

Example: Right now I rent an apartment, but I wish I owned a house.

1. ________________________________

2. ________________________________

3. ________________________________

4. ________________________________

5. ________________________________

Study Skills and Strategies: Adding Factual Information

A. Complete the caption under the photograph. Try first without looking back at the story on pages 93–94 of your textbook. Then check to see if you were correct.

The Friendship Bridge, which connects

____________________________________,

was completed in 1994.

B. To help readers understand more about a topic, writers sometimes add factual information within a sentence. One way of doing this is to add a **nonrestrictive relative clause** after a noun. These types of relative clauses add extra information; they are not essential to the meaning of the sentence.

Nonrestrictive Relative Clauses
The King of Thailand, **who had never visited Laos,** walked across the bridge to greet the President of Laos. The Mekong River, **which flows through Laos, Cambodia, and Vietnam**, is one of the world's longest rivers.
Nonrestrictive relative clauses add extra information about a topic, but are not essential to the general meaning of the sentence. Nonrestrictive relative clauses begin with *who* or *which*, and are set off from the rest of the sentence with commas (,)

In the sentence you completed under the photograph, which part is the relative clause? What extra information does it tell the reader? Write the relative clause here:

____

C. Add factual information from the box to the following sentences.

> Los Angeles has a population of about 3,485,000.
>
> Ronald Reagan was governor of California from 1966 to 1974.
>
> Thousands of Vietnamese refugees immigrated to California after 1975.

1. Los Angeles, ____,
is the biggest city in California.

2. Ronald Reagan, ____,
became the fortieth president of the U.S. at the age of 69.

3. Thousands of Vietnamese refugees, _________________________,
have homes and business in an area south of Los Angeles known as "Little Saigon."

Study Skills and Strategies: Recognizing Time and Sequence Clues

A. Read the following sentences that describe the Hmong people of Laos. Identify each sentence as one of the following.

1. General descriptions of Hmong culture.
2. Descriptions of historical events.
3. Description of the current situation.

_______ Hmong culture, which is over 4,000 years old, places high value on freedom and loyalty.

_______ In the nineteenth century, thousands of Hmong migrated from their homes in southern China into the mountains of Laos.

_______ For 200 years, the Hmong lived peacefully with other ethnic minorities, as well as with the majority lowland Lao, who lived in the fertile river valleys.

_______ During the war in Southeast Asia, the United States recruited Hmong soldiers to fight against the Vietnamese and the Pathet Lao forces in Laos.

_______ After the United States pulled out of Southeast Asia, thousands of Hmong refugees escaped to camps in Thailand.

_______ For centuries, the Hmong have expressed their history, legends, and beliefs in their art, especially in the design of jewelry and needlework.

_______ Today, Hmong women living in the United States continue to tell their stories in the form of colorful designs and tapestries, which they sell in craft shops and open air markets.

B. Choose one sentence from each category you identified. For each sentence, look at the time words or phrases that help you understand the time frame of each description. Identify the main verb. Write this information in the chart below.

Category	Time Word/Phrase	Main Verb
1		
2		
3		

C. Written descriptions often begin with a general statement about the topic. Using a sentence from Category #1 as a model, write an introductory sentence about your culture or country.

____

____

More Reading and Writing: *Native Country:* Memories of Vietnam

A. "Native Country" is a Vietnamese song. As you read the words, think about the images the writer uses to communicate his childhood memories of Vietnam. How might the song help Vietnamese-Americans stay in touch with their own memories.

My native country was a bunch of sweet star fruit
I usually gathered every day.
My native country was the road back from school
With plenty of yellow butterflies.
My native country was my blue kite, in my boyhood
I ran over the rice fields to fly it up into the sky.
My native country was a small boat, drifting smoothly
Along the riverside,
My native country was the small bamboo bridge,
My mother wearing her latamier leaf hat walked
Over it to go back home.
My native country was the full moon nights
People could see the white areca flowers fall
around the house.
Everyone has one homeland, like he has only
One mother.
Those who forget this can never grow up.

Translated by Ba Tu

B. Underline ten things in the song that remind the writer of his homeland.

C. Think of one thing that "takes you back" to your childhood and the place where you were born. This may be an image you remember, or something you still have. It may also be a food, a smell, or a sound. Complete this line of the song with your own memory.

My native country was ______________________________________.

D. On a separate sheet of paper, describe your memory in detail. Use words to paint a picture of the place for someone who has never been there.

Vocabulary Review: Major Life Events

A. Many of the important events in a person's life can be expressed in at least two ways: as a verb or verb phrase (graduated, was born) or as a noun or noun phrase (birth, graduation, birth of a daughter). Think of the important events that have occurred (and you expect to occur) in your life. Change the verbs to nouns, and write them on the lines outside the circle. Add more events or substitute different ones if you wish.

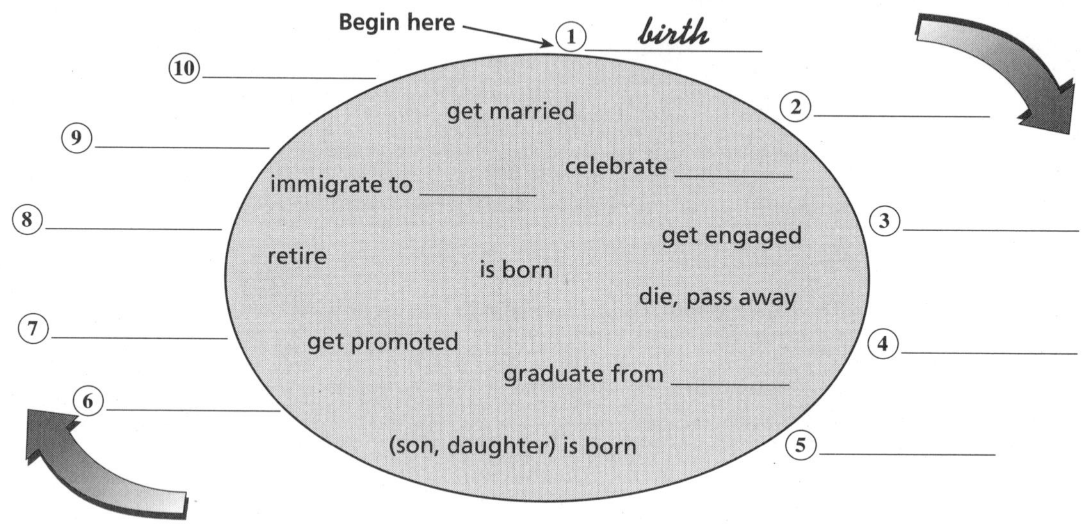

B. Complete these sentences, using appropriate words or phrases from inside or around the circle. Add endings to the verb forms if necessary.

1. Tsegyi Dolma was ____born____ in 1959.
2. One of the best days of her life was the day of her ________________ from nursing school.
3. My parents ________________ their fiftieth wedding anniversary last year.
4. The date of their ________________ to this country was 1948.
5. Maria has worked hard all her life, but she doesn't want to ________________ yet.

C. Which of the major events in *your* life do you feel has been important? In a sentence or two, briefly describe what happened and why it is important to you.

____

____

Test Yourself

Circle or fill in the correct answers.

1. Writing letters, ______________________, and going back for visits are good ways of staying in touch.

   a) photographs b) send photographs c) sending photographs

2. When you send international mail, the last line of the address must show only ______________________.

   a) the ZIP code b) the country name c) the street address

3. If you wanted to invite your teacher to a wedding, you would probably send a ______________________.

   a) note b) descriptive essay c) formal invitation

4. If you have any questions, please ______________________.

   a) give me a call, OK? b) call the guy in my office. c) do not hesitate to contact me.

5. If they hadn't immigrated to America, they wouldn't ______________________ to speak English.

   a) have learned b) had learn c) have learn

6. If Saisana lived in California, he might ______________________ a typical American teenager.

   a) been b) being c) be

7. Hmong culture, ______________________ is over 4,000 years old, places high value on freedom and loyalty.

   a) which b) that c) who

8. Today, Hmong women living in the United States ______________________ to tell their stories.

   a) continuing b) continue c) continued

9. They got engaged last week and hope to ______________________ soon.

   a) marriage b) get married c) get marriage

10. Her date of ______________________ is August 14, 1958.

    a) born b) birth c) was born

Language Learning Diary

A. Think about the ways people stay in touch with their relatives and friends in different parts of the world **and** about the English you have learned in this unit. Using some of the prompts in the box as guides, write about what you've learned and would like to learn.

I learned about . . .
I spoke English to . . .
I listened to . . .
I read about . . .
I wrote about . . .
The strategies I used are . . .
I want to learn more about . . .

____

____

____

____

____

____

____

____

____

B. New words and phrases I want to remember. Keep a record of when you see, hear, or use a new word or phrase from this unit outside the classroom.

Word/Phrase	I saw it . . .	I heard it . . .	I used it . . .
for good	______________	on a TV show	at a friend's house: I was talking about my future plans

ANSWER KEY • • •

Unit 1 • • •

page 2: A. Answers will vary, but possibilities include descriptive adjectives (wealthy, wise), noun phrases (a Buddhist, a business-woman), or adjective + relative clause combinations (satisfied with my life).

B. Answers will vary.

page 3: B. Answers will vary, but possibilities include:
1. He is retired.
2. He is very busy.
3. His poetry is popular.

C. Answers will vary.

page 4: A.
1. We have two sons who help us run this business.
2. My husband is a hard worker who never wants to retire.
3. I enjoy spending time with friends who like to sing and tell stories in Arabic.

B. Answers will vary.

page 6: A. and B. Answers will vary.

page 7: A. Answers will vary.

B. Answers will vary, but possibilities include:
I'm good at singing, but I'm not very talented at writing poetry.

page 8: B. Answers will vary.

C. Answers will vary, but possibilities include:
date of birth—1957
country of birth—Cuba

page 9: C. Answers will vary. Check for use of five preposition clusters.

page 10: A.
1. <u>is called</u>
2. <u>was published</u>
3. <u>were granted</u>
4. <u>was established</u>
5. <u>are used</u>

B. Answers will vary, but possibilities include:
It is called "Two Countries."
It was written by Mariano Ramos.

page 11: A.
1. F
2. O
3. F
4. F
5. O

B. Check for statement of opinion and use at least one supporting fact or example.

page 12: A. Answers will vary.

B.
1. Answers will vary.
2. Check for full statement of opinion.

page 13: 1. a 2. c 3. a 4. c 5. b 6. a 7. c 8. a 9. a 10. a

Unit 2 • • •

page 16: Answers will vary.

page 17: Answers will vary.

page 18: A. Answers can vary somewhat but will be similar to the following:
1. My friend <u>had been studying</u> English <u>for about six months</u> before she came to the United States.
2. Some students in the class <u>had been speaking</u> English fluently <u>for many years</u> before they began to study in class.

3. Because the woman was a good student, she had been reviewing her notes for three hours before the examination.
4. One man said that he had been learning English since 1992.
5. When I called my friend, he said that he had been writing in his journal for half an hour.

B. Answers will vary.

page 19: A. Answers will vary.

B. Answers will vary.

page 20: Answers will vary but be similar to these examples: decelerate, disagreeable, bookish, comical, divisible, disembark, employment, disengage, hostility, reintroduce, retype, coworker

page 21: B. Answers will vary

page 22: A. 1. S 2. M 3. M 4. S 5. M 6. M 7. S 8. M

B. Answers will vary.

page 23: Answers will vary.

page 24: A. Answers will vary.

B. Answers will vary.

page 25: 1. b 2. c 3. c 4. a 5. b 6. a 7. c 8. b 9. a

page 26: A. Answers will vary.

B. Answers will vary.

Unit 3 • • •

page 28: A. 2. For the next two years I didn't talk to my parents.
3. I would come home from school, eat dinner, go to my room to do school work, and then go to bed.

B. 2. Answers will vary.
3. Answers will vary.

page 29: A. 2. c 3. b 4. a 5. f 6. d

B. 2. went out on
3. find out
4. gave in
5. catching on
6. come over

C. Answers will vary.

page 30: B. 2. He said she could not marry a poor refugee.
3. My mother said that she had her career.
4. She said she would not marry anyone else.
5. She said marriage is not important to her so she would not get married

C. Answers will vary.

page 31: B. end a relationship = break up
search = look for
be careful = watch out
to succeed = work out

C. Answers will vary.

page 32: A. Physical Appearance: handsome; tall; beautiful; attractive
Personality: flexible; trustworthy; sense of humor; patient; kind
Other: educated; rich; religion; from my culture; good cook; good job

page 33: A. 6; 1; 7; 11; 2; 9; 5; 3; 10; 4; 8

B. 1. 7:30
2. yes
3. ?

page 34: B. 1. more Americans are waiting longer to get married
2. The Census Bureau Started collecting statistics more than 100 years ago.

C. Answers will vary.

page 35: B. 1. The ages of American men and women when they get married.
2. 1890–1990
3. In 1940 men were marrying at an earlier age than in 1960
4. Why the age of the first marriage had changed

page 36: A. Nouns: February 14; Valentine's Day: love; custom; Roman Empire; Romans; celebration; February 15; Lupercalia; day; girls; names; box; man; girlfriend; year; legends; birds; mates; Catholic Church; saints; Valentine; relationship; Saint Valentines; lovers; century; people; cards; boxes; chocolates; flowers; jewelry; relatives; friends
Verbs: known; is; to celebrate; believe; dates; had; called; put; take out; to find; is told; choose; honors; named; began; give; become; to tell; are
Adjectives: special; old; young; next; other; several; popular; heart-shaped

page 37: 1. b 2. a 3. b 4. c 5. a 6. b 7. c 8. b

Unit 4 • • •

page 40: B. Answers will vary but will include some of the following words: well-qualified, friendly, positive attitude, flexible, cooperative, diligent, like working with people, have high energy, have enthusiasm, creative

C. Answers will vary.

page 41: A. Answers will vary.

B. Answers will vary.

page 42–43: Answers will vary.

page 44–45: Answers will vary.

page 47: Answers will vary.

page 48:

page 49: A. work, have, work, don't like, find, tell, decide, should get, travel, needs, is

B. Answers will vary.

page 50: Answers will vary.

page 51: 1. c 2. a 3. b 4. a 5. c 6. c 7. b 8. b 9. b

page 52: A. Answers will vary.

B. Answers will vary.

Unit 5 • • •

page 54: A. Answers will vary.

B. Answers will vary.

C. Answers will vary but possible answers include:
1. Where is Jubilee?
2. When did Don Mosley and his family come to Jubilee?
3. Where did he read about the boat people of Vietnam?
4. How many refugees have come to Jubilee?
5. Where did the first refugees come from?
6. What is Jubilee's official goal?
7. What other things does Jubilee do?

page 55:

A. ed: excited; congested; relaxed; polluted
y: hilly; windy; cloudy; stormy; foggy; breezy; noisy
ful: peaceful
ous: mountainous
al: natural

B. Answers will vary.

C. Answers will vary.

page 56:

A. shocked; comfortable; nicest period of my life in the United States; peaceful; helpful

B. Paragraph 1: Nermina's feelings about Jubilee.
Paragraph 2: Studying at Jubilee.
Paragraph 3: Nermina wants to study in Atlanta but she'll have to wait for her brother.

C. Answers will vary.

D. Answers will vary.

page 59:

1. Automatic teller machine
2. Personal identification number
3. So no one else can use your card.
4. Report a lost card.
5. Stand in a position so no one else can see your transaction.
6. Answers will vary.

page 61:

1. Persons who performed volunteer work in 1989.
2. Characteristic of the volunteers.
3. Women did more volunteer work.
4. 25 to 34
5. 16.8%
6. Answers will vary.

page 62:

B. first; and; but; also; because; therefore

C. 1. Refugee 2. volunteer 3. partner 4. refugee host

D. moreover; but; because; and; for

page 65:

1. b 2. a 3. c 4. b 5. c 6. b 7. c 8. c

Unit 6 • • •

page 68:

B. Answers will vary.

page 70:

B. 1. Letters and Letter Packages
2. Small Packets
3. Printed Matter
4. Small Packets or Parcel Post
5. Aerogrammes

page 71:

B. Sample D
Sample B
Sample A
Sample E
Sample C

page 72:

C. Sample A: personal narrative
Sample B: personal note
Sample C: descriptive essay
Sample D: formal invitation
Sample E: formal letter

D. 1. personal note
2. descriptive essay
3. formal letter
4. personal narrative
5. formal invitation

page 73:

A. Answers will vary. Check for correct grammatical form.

page 74:

B. Answers will vary.

C. Answers will vary. Check for correct grammatical form.

page 75:

B. which connects Laos and Thailand

C. 1. which has a population of about 3,485,000
2. who was governor of California from 1966 to 1974.
3. who immigrated to California after 1975.

page 76:

A. 1, 2, 2, 2, 2, 1, 3

page 78:

A. Order will vary, but noun forms include:
birth, graduation, celebration, engagement, retirement, death

B. 1. born
2. graduation
3. celebrated
4. immigration
5. retire

page 79: 1. c 2. b 3. c 4. c 5. a 6. c 7. a 8. b 9. b 10. b